Micro-computers in Personnel

Michael Norman graduated from Sheffield University in 1963 with a BSc (Special Honours) in Mathematics. After working for four years as an Operational Research scientist at Shell-Mex and BP he went to Toronto University where he attained an MASc in Industrial Engineering. He stayed in Canada for a further three years, working for Price Waterhouse Associates. When he returned to England in 1973 he joined Wootton, Jeffreys and Partners where he became an Associate. In 1980 he formed his own company, M.J.N. Consulting Limited. He specializes in advising organizations on their computer requirements, particularly in the personnel area, and has led a team developing a micro-computer based personnel system. He also lectures on computer applications to businessmen and gives lecture courses on management science and systems analysis to undergraduates and postgraduates.

Tim Edwards graduated from the University of Wales Institute of Science and Technology with a BSc (Tech) in Occupational Psychology. After a sabbatical year as President of the students union he began his career in personnel management with J Sainsbury. In 1979 he joined the Tarmac group of companies and was involved with the development of a micro-computer personnel and payroll administration system for Tarmac Building Products. During 1983 he moved to Lloyds Bowmaker Finance Group. Following his first-hand experience in the problems of introducing a micro-computer system, Tim Edwards presented a case study to the Second National Conference on Computers in Personnel and has spoken on the subject at several IPM branch meetings.

The authors jointly present seminars for the Institute of Personnel Management and the Industrial Society on the application of micro-computers.

Micro·computers in Personnel

Michael Norman
Tim Edwards

The Institute of Personnel Management

Note: wherever appropriate the convention
has been followed whereby *he* and *him*
are used to cover *she* and *her*.

Printed and bound in Great Britain
by R. J. Acford, Chichester, Sussex

British Library Cataloguing in Publication Data
Microcomputers in personnel.
1. Personnel management — Data processing
2. Microcomputers
I. Title   II. Edwards, Tim
658.3'0028'5404   HF 5549
ISBN 0-85292-334-1

Contents

List of figures

Acknowledgements

The authors are indebted to many people who, individually or collectively, have helped in the preparation of this book. We would first like to thank the companies who have allowed their experiences in installing and using a micro-computer based personnel system to be put on record. Without their contributions the book would have been restricted to theoretical musings.

A great debt is due to Bridget Norman and Christine Stone who laboured over our manuscripts and produced the typed proofs for the printer.

Finally, we would like to thank Sally Harper, Fiona Murchie and Steve West for their help and guidance throughout the writing and production of the book.

Introduction

'We live in a moment of history where change is so speeded up that we begin to see the present only when it is already disappearing.'
Laing R D. *The Politics of Experience*. Penguin Books, 1967

In recent years a revolution has taken place in office administration and many organizations have considered the use of computers to improve their efficiency. Until recently, the only computer systems available were those designed for large computers. These were often very expensive and cumbersome to use and managers were reluctant to devote time and resources to mastering them. The advent of micro-computers has changed all that, providing an opportunity to secure cheap but powerful aids to business efficiency. There are numerous computer systems available and choosing the right one for a particular application can be a daunting task. This book is designed to help personnel administrators in this very difficult appraisal.

Until the mid-1960s most offices were equipped with typewriters, filing cabinets, reams of writing pads and pre-printed forms. In general no computing devices other than desk calculators were employed. Gradually organizations introduced large central computers and working patterns began to change. In time some of the pre-printed forms became documents for the input of data to the central computer and many man-hours were spent transcribing words and numbers on to the documents and then on to a medium such as punched cards for input to the computer.

The next innovation (around 1970) was the arrival of word processors which are machines capable of reducing the time taken significantly to prepare letters, reports and other business documents. Clearly they have many advantages but acceptance of word processing has been gradual and not without a considerable amount of resistance from both users and administrators.

Similar resistance is being shown to the introduction of micro-computers which have the ability to perform many diverse functions, including word processing. This resistance is understandable, especially as the 'beast' is actually present in the office instead of being hidden away in a data processing department. The very accessibility of micro-computers is their greatest asset since the user no longer has to beg a remote bureaucracy to provide some data, and then wait for its arrival. The information can be available immediately.

Advances in technology have meant that smaller computers can now carry out tasks previously the preserve of larger and more expensive machines. Consequently there is a strong trend towards the use of smaller computers and recent surveys have confirmed that this trend is equally as prevalent within personnel departments. There are racks of magazines that describe and review computers and their associated equipment, and exhibitions are mounted all over the country. The array of choices is bewildering and the potential buyer would be forgiven for not knowing where to start looking.

This book has been written to give the personnel administrator with no expert knowledge of computers a rounded view of the subject. It will also assist computer departments in assessing the requirements of the personnel function. Hopefully, reading the book will provide not only an understanding of micro-computers and their capabilities but also an appreciation of what would be the best type of system to meet individual requirements.

It is as well, at this point, to describe what is meant by the term micro-computer (or 'micro') although a much fuller explanation is given in chapter 2 which deals with the whole subject of computers and their functions and operations. A micro is a low-cost computer that normally sits on an office desk but can perform many of the functions available on a large computer installation. The machine will usually be for use by one person at a time and be independent of other office equipment. Many business micros, however, will have the ability to serve several users and to communicate with other computers.

Computer programs to aid the personnel administrator are also numerous and chapter 3 describes the various types available. Examples of their application are given with suggestions for using them to the best advantage.

A very important aspect of the subject is determining how a micro-computer system should be used. Chapter 4 describes a step by step approach to ensuring that a system realizes its full potential.

The case studies reveal how two companies, operating in different environments, approached the administrative problems of personnel work. One opted for an integrated payroll and personnel system whilst the other concentrated on straightforward personnel record keeping.

Finally, a glossary of computing terms is given to aid the potential user in understanding articles and advertisements describing computers and computer systems. The bibliography gives details of recommended books for further reading together with a list of some of the more popular computer magazines.

1 :: Taking the first step

Introduction

The world of computing can be totally baffling to anyone who has not had the time, or perhaps the inclination, to study it in depth and personnel managers are often in that position. However, the burden of administration can become so heavy that they feel the need to explore the possibilities of using a computer to assist them in that task. Having taken that step they may then discover that a computer could not only remove some of the drudgery associated with their role but it could also be an aid to the more creative tasks such as personnel development, manpower planning etc.

The real problem then is to choose the right system. This book has been written to help the reader in his research and as a guide to making a sensible choice of computer and personnel system. The book concentrates on micro-computer systems since they are readily available, easy to use and relatively inexpensive.

Hardware and software

A computerized system is made up of the machinery itself (hardware) and the programs that make the machinery perform the required tasks (software). It is not necessary for a personnel administrator to have a deep knowledge of micro-computers and their workings but it is essential that they know sufficient to be able to make sensible choices of the hardware and software.

The micro-computer hardware has several essential components:

the central processing unit containing the controlling func-

1

tions, the arithmetic and logic unit and internal (working) storage memory

at least one visual display unit, which together with a keyboard provides the user with the means to communicate with the central processing unit

floppy or hard discs to provide permanent storage for programs and data

at least one printer for the production of reports and letters.

Optional extras include: single sheet feeders, acoustic hoods and special stands for printers; communications equipment for transmitting data to and from remote locations; and special printing equipment for graphical output.

Each item of equipment has to be chosen so that it can satisfy current and expected requirements, although it should be possible to buy a basic system that is capable of being extended as and when necessary.

The most important but the most difficult task is to choose the right programs (software) whether they are written especially for the user, bought as a package from a dealer or prepared as a combination of the two.

Programs are available for a variety of personnel tasks:

personnel record keeping

personnel administration, ie record keeping combined with complex enquiries and reporting

absence recording

administration of statutory sick pay

payroll

pensions administration

recruitment

personnel development and training

manpower planning.

Very few systems encompassing all these tasks in one suite of programs would be available, even on a main-frame; certainly, none exists on a micro-computer. Potential users have to decide which of these tasks they wish to be carried out within a single micro-computer system and which they would be happy to see performed separately. There are many advantages to be obtained from combining several tasks into an integrated system but no hard and fast fules can be laid down since each organization has different operating methods and requirements.

Choosing a system

The first step towards procuring a computerized personnel system is usually taken when a personnel manager comes to the conclusion that 'something must be done' to ease the administrative load on his department. There may be a strong temptation to rush out and buy a micro-computer and then see what it can do and how it can help. This temptation should be resisted! Having decided that a computer could be of assistance the personnel manager should then enumerate all the tasks that he would like the computer to perform, either fully or partially. To a large extent this will determine which pieces of data are to be stored on the computer but it is also a useful exercise to make a comprehensive list of both the necessary information and also that which could be usefully stored if practicable. Finally, and most importantly, a series of schedules detailing how the system would be used should be drawn up. All this is encapsulated in

Rule 1: decide what the system is to be used for
The stage is now set for the search for a system, bearing in mind

Rule 2: choose the software first and then the hardware
Most organizations will already have a computer of some sort, usually a main-frame in the larger organizations. The suppliers of that computer could be the first port of call for the personnel manager but it is essential to observe

Rule 3: research the market
Advice can be obtained from many quarters: internal data processing department; internal management scientists; outside consultants; and personnel departments in other organizations. It will also be helpful for the personnel manager, or a designated

3

member of his staff, to read some of the computer magazines, particularly those which give lists of micro-computers and the packages available for them.

Last, and by no means least

Rule 4: consider future requirements
It is important to choose a system that can grow both in storage capacity, to accommodate more employee records or more information per employee, and in the number of users that can have access to the system.

The experience of the two companies who provided the case studies set out in chapters 5 and 6 should provide some guidance for personnel managers embarking on a similar exercise. However, no two organizations have identical needs and it is important to understand that considerable detailed research will have to be carried out before a system can be chosen with confidence.

Installing the system

Once the new system has been chosen, the personnel department can prepare for its installation. The preparations fall into four categories:

physical requirements

training of staff

data transfer

provision for maintenance and support.

Security considerations will probably determine where the computer will be housed, but the VDUs and printer may not be in the same room. Consequently, cables will have to be run through the offices and care will be needed to stop these becoming unsightly or even, dangerous. Printers are noisy and should either be housed in a separate room or a good quality acoustic hood should be acquired. The personnel staff who will be using the new system should be fully briefed as to what will be arriving and what it will be doing. Ideally, they should have been fully consulted during the early stages of the project so that their suggestions for program features, preferred type of vdu etc could have been taken into consideration.

The most time consuming task that has to be undertaken concerns the transfer of data from manual records or an existing computer system. It is most common for the time taken for this operation to be seriously underestimated (see, for example, the case study in chapter 5).

Finally, adequate arrangements should be made to ensure that the hardware and software are fully maintained and that the users know who to contact should there be any queries.

Future developments

The rapid growth in the use of micro-computers will necessarily have an impact on working patterns within personnel departments. First, there will be a continuing trend to transfer information from pieces of paper to computer discs and microfiche. Although this could lead to greater confidentiality of data, some employees and personnel managers will fear that this move will have the opposite effect. Data protection legislation has been introduced to control the use of personal data and to ensure that it is not misused. However there are areas within personnel management, particularly in employee development, where its impact is not yet fully defined.

The second change in working arrangements is concerned with flexibility in location and hours of work. It is already possible for a personnel administrator to take a micro-computer home to work on in the evening. It will soon be commonplace for some employees to work at home during the day and to use computers or terminals to communicate with their colleagues at the office or at their homes. The movement away from centralized work places may not be as pronounced for personnel administrators as with other groups of workers; nevertheless, it will still be a factor to take into account.

Predicting the future is fraught with pitfalls but it can be stated confidently that micro-computers will play an ever increasing role in personnel administration. The trend will be to smaller, cheaper, and more powerful machines linked to each other and, where necessary, to a centralized installation. A generation is growing up who will take this in their stride. The challenge is to instruct and train today's personnel managers in the use and potential of these ubiquitous machines.

2 :: Micro-computers

Introduction

Computers are essentially simple machines capable of carrying out complicated tasks. Unfortunately, most people harbour misconceptions of what they are and how they work. The problem is compounded when considering micro-computers (more commonly referred to as micros) since so much has been written and spoken about them in the popular media. Regrettably many of the statements in the media are either misleading or plainly wrong. Consequently it will be helpful for the reader to have a basic appreciation of micros and their workings.

Development of computers

The recording of business transactions is as old as history. For example, pictographic writing on clay tablets dating back to the Sumerians of 3,000 BC have been recovered, and various developments in record keeping can be traced through the Babylonian and Assyrian cultures to the orderly bookkeeping of the Greeks and Romans. The medium for storing data has progressed from the early materials to modern paper and, more recently, to electronic machinery. Similarly, the recording instruments have developed from sharp stones to pencils, pens and typewriter keyboards.

The mere recording of data is rarely an end in itself and the more interesting procedure is the manipulation of the data to provide useful information. The earliest calculator of any sophistication was the abacus, invented by the Chinese over 4,500 years ago. Amazingly, no notable progress in design was made

7

until the seventeenth century with the development of logarithms, slide rules and gear-driven adding machines. Perhaps the most significant invention was that of the punched card which formed the basis of the design for Jacquard's loom. This marvellous machine facilitated the automatic control of a textile loom using a continuous band of the punched cards which enabled the loom to perform one task at a time in a pre-set sequence. This was the inspiration for Charles Babbage who, in 1812, devised an 'analytical engine' which in concept closely resembled the design of modern computers. Unfortunately Babbage was too far ahead of his time and the engine proved impossible to construct.

The development of the modern computer really began during the Second World War when a team of American scientists built a series of relay calculators for use by the US forces. The first commercial computer was introduced at the beginning of the 1950s and during that decade businesses and government departments took delivery of a number of these enormous machines. The early machines, which used vacuum valves to store the data, were termed the 'first generation computers' and the introduction of solid state transistors in the mid-1950s heralded the arrival of the second generation. The third generation is represented by microminitiarization (even smaller electronic components) and the development of integrated circuits etched on small slices of silicon or germanium (the silicon chip).

How computers work

Although computers are complicated pieces of machinery, their basic design is logical and quite straightforward. To understand this, consider how the human brain performs a simple calculation. Suppose that the date is Wednesday, 2 May 1984, and the date of the Thursday in the following week is wanted. The brain will quickly calculate that the answer is 10 May 1984 – but how does it do it? First, the initial information – Wednesday and 2 – has to be retained. (For the purposes of this illustration 'May' and '1984' will be discarded from the discussion.) Secondly, the number of days in a week (7) needs to be known and also that Wednesday comes one day before Thursday. And, thirdly, an ability to add numbers is required.

8

In addition, there is a need for a controlling mechanism to make it all work and a means of storing intermediate results (9, in our example, being the number obtained by adding 2 and 7). These control and storage functions form, together with ways of receiving (input) and transmitting (output) data, the basis of computer design. Figure 1 below illustrates this.

In the example, 'Wednesday' and '2' enter the store from the *input* device (ear). This store already has the information '7 days in a week' and 'Thursday follows Wednesday'. The *control unit* pulls all the information together and instructs the *arithmetic and logic unit* (ALU) to add 7 to 2 (= 9) and add 1 (= 10) to achieve the result, which is then passed to the store for subsequent *output* (via the mouth).

Naturally, computers are designed to perform generalized calculations and not just to work out the date of the next Thursday. To this end, the *instructions* (eg 'add 7 to 2') need to be changeable so that other calculations can be performed. This is achieved by enabling the store to remember instructions as well as *data*. A set of such instructions is called a *program* (traditionally spelt this way in the computer world) and a general purpose machine is called a *stored program computer*.

Figure 1
Outline of a computer system

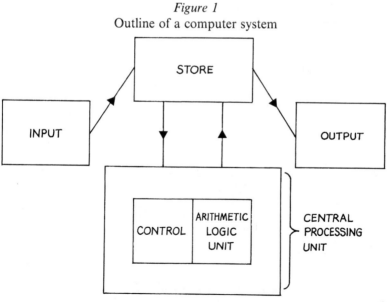

Before looking at the operations of a computer, it is necessary to digress for a moment to consider how data is stored and transmitted. Within a computer, each component can be considered as either 'on' or 'off' – transistors are conducting or not conducting; magnetic materials are magnetized or not magnetized; switches are open or closed; voltages are present or not present. If 'on' is represented by '1' and 'off' by '0' then the representation is called *binary notation*.

To understand binary numbers, such as 110101, consider the decimal number 2566. This number can be represented as shown in figure 2 below. The representation of the equivalent binary number is given in figure 3 below. Note that the principles are the same although more positions are required for the binary number.

Figure 2

Decimal representation of a number

10^5	10^4	10^3	10^2	10^1	10^0
100000	10000	1000	100	10	1
2	5	6	6		

$$6 \times 1 = 6$$
$$6 \times 10 = 60$$
$$5 \times 100 = 500$$
$$2 \times 1000 = 2000$$
$$\overline{2566}$$

Note: 10^4 is a short form for $10 \times 10 \times 10 \times 10$ ($= 10000$)
10^0 is a traditional representation for 1

Figure 3

Binary representation of a number

2^{12}	2^{11}	2^{10}	2^9	2^8	2^7	2^6	2^5	2^4	2^3	2^2	2^1	2^0
4096	2048	1024	512	256	128	64	32	16	8	4	2	1
1	0	1	0	0	0	0	0	0	1	1	0	

$$1 \times 2 = 2$$
$$1 \times 4 = 4$$
$$1 \times 512 = 512$$
$$1 \times 2048 = 2048$$
$$\overline{2566}$$

Addition of binary numbers (ie numbers to the base 2) follows the same rules as addition of decimal numbers (ie numbers to the base 10). For example,

in decimal:

$34 + 19$
$$= 30 + 4 + 10 + 9$$
$$= 30 + 10 + 4 + 9$$
$$= 30 + 10 + 10 + 3$$
$$= 53$$

in binary:

$100010 + 10011 = 100000 + 10 + 10000 + 10 + 1$
$$= 100000 + 10000 + 10 + 10 + 1$$
$$= 100000 + 10000 + 100 + 1$$
$$= 110101$$

Returning to the decription of the internal workings of a computer, the first element is the *store* which is split into equal-sized *locations*. Each of these locations (also called *addresses*) consists of a pattern of binary digits, eg 110101. These addresses can be thought of as pigeon holes into which numbers, letters or internal computer instructions are stored. The jargon for binary digits is *bits*. Confusingly a group of binary digits, or bits, is called a *byte* and is the smallest unit capable of storing numbers, letters (both upper and lower case) and special characters, such as *.

There are a variety of ways in which patterns of bits can be used to represent letters and symbols. The two code sets most commonly used in computing are EBCDIC (Extended Binary Coded Decimal Interchange Code) and ASCII (American Standard Code for Information Interchange). EBCDIC is an eight bit (one byte) code, each bit position having a specific meaning, as shown in figure 4 on page 12.

As an example, the letter M would be represented in EBCDIC as follows:

M:	1	1	0	1	0	1	0	0
	upper case letters		J to R		4 – because M is the fourth letter in the sequence J to R			

The word MICRO would be represented by five bytes and, in EBCDIC, the bit patterns would be as shown in figure 5 on page 12.

Figure 4
The EBCDIC coding system

Bit position:	Zone bits				Numeric bits			
	0	1	2	3	4	5	6	7
	Symbol Indicators		Alphabetic/ Numeric Indicators		Digits 0 to 9			
bit	upper case letters 1	1	A to I 0	0	0	0	0	0
					0	0	0	1
bit	lower case letters 1	0	J to R 0	1	0	0	1	0
					0	0	1	1
					0	1	0	0
					0	1	0	1
bit	special characters 0	1	S to Z 1	0	0	1	1	0
					0	1	1	1
					1	0	0	0
					1	0	0	1
bit	unassigned 0	0	numbers 1	1				

Figure 5
Representation of word MICRO in the EBCDIC code

M:	1	1	0	1	0	1	0	0
I:	1	1	0	0	1	0	0	1
C:	1	1	0	0	0	0	1	1
R:	1	1	0	1	1	0	0	1
O:	1	1	0	1	0	1	1	0

Numbers, letters and symbols are transmitted from one part of the computer to another by means of electronic pulses. These pulses are grouped in patterns, in the same way as bit patterns, to form messages. In this manner, each part of the computer can communicate with any other part.

12

The complete (upper case) alphabet and numbers in the EBCDIC and ASCII codes are given in figure 6 on page 14.

Stores are either *read from* (contents copied to the processor or output device) or *written to* (data or instructions put to store). These actions take time, known as *response time*. Also, the store will be of a finite size or *capacity*. These two measurements together determine some of the more important characteristics of the computer, in the same way that efficiency and size affect the choice of a car.

Proceeding to the arithmetic and logic unit (ALU), consider the operation of adding two numbers. First, the ALU needs to know the storage addresses of the two numbers and the address in which to place the result. This could be represented by 'ADD (x,y,z)', where x and y are the addresses of the original numbers and z is the address of the result. 'ADD' is known as the *operator* and x, y and z are known as the *operand addresses*. If, as in the original example, it is required to add 2 to 7 and these numbers are in locations 20 and 21 respectively and if the answer is to be put into location 22, the instruction would read 'ADD (20,21,22)'.

An instruction of the form ADD (20,21,22) is rather clumsy and computers usually use a format that involves a single address only. To achieve this, more operators and a partial result store, known as an *accumulator*, are required. The instructions could then read:

LOAD ACCUMULATOR   with contents of location 20
ADD to number in accumulator   contents of location 21
STORE result   as the contents of location 22

In shorthand,
    LDA20
    ADD21
    STO22

A fundamental aspect of computer design concerns the choice of *word length*, where a 'word' is the collection of bits necessary to represent both numbers and instructions (which also have to be stored). In the representation of numbers, one bit is reserved for the sign (ie whether it is positive or negative) and so a 16-bit word will have 15 positions for the actual number. The largest number available is 111111111111111, or 32767.

Words to describe instructions are divided into two sections,

Figure 6

Numbers and upper case letters in the ABCDIC and ASCII codes

CHARACTER	EBCDIC		ASCII	
0	1111	0000	011	0000
1	1111	0001	011	0001
2	1111	0010	011	0010
3	1111	0011	011	0011
4	1111	0100	011	0100
5	1111	0101	011	0101
6	1111	0110	011	0110
7	1111	0111	011	0111
8	1111	1000	011	1000
9	1111	1001	011	1001
A	1100	0001	100	0001
B	1100	0010	100	0010
C	1100	0011	100	0011
D	1100	0100	100	0100
E	1100	0101	100	0101
F	1100	0110	100	0110
G	1100	0111	100	0111
H	1100	1000	100	1000
I	1100	1001	100	1001
J	1101	0001	100	1010
K	1101	0010	100	1011
L	1101	0011	100	1100
M	1101	0100	100	1101
N	1101	0101	100	1110
O	1101	0110	100	1111
P	1101	0111	101	0000
Q	1101	1000	101	0001
R	1101	1001	101	0010
S	1110	0010	101	0011
T	1110	0011	101	0100
U	1110	0100	101	0101
V	1110	0101	101	0110
W	1110	0110	101	0111
X	1110	0111	101	1000
Y	1110	1000	101	1001
Z	1110	1001	101	1010

one each for operator and operand address. The choice of word length is then determined by the sum of the two section lengths. For the operator section 4 bits (giving a total of 15 functions) is usually sufficient, and 12 further bits (allowing 4095 addresses) completes the 16-bit word.

The limitations on number size and the number of addresses can be overcome by clever computing algorithms that are outside the scope of this book.

Definition of a micro-computer

The early computers covered large amounts of floor area and consisted of many cabinets full of electronic gadgetry. The cabinet that housed the arithmetic logic unit (ALU) – the heart of the machine – was called the 'main-frame' and this name has stuck to describe large computers. Modern main-frames are very expensive and very powerful; they can serve many users and perform many tasks simultaneously. The early 1970s saw the introduction of smaller, less powerful but very much cheaper 'mini-computers' (minis). Although there was still the demand for main-frames, many organizations saw the mini as both adequate and affordable.

EXAMPLES OF LARGER COMPUTERS

Main-frames	Minis
IBM 360/370	Prime 350/450
ICL 1900 Series	DEC 11/34, VAX
Univac	Hewlett Packard 3000
CDC 6000	Honeywell
	IBM System 34
	ICL ME29

The arrival of the micro has been as dramatic as the introduction of the first main-frame computer but the effects have been much more visible. Not only are micros carrying out tasks formerly assigned to minis, and even main-frames, but they are also appearing in many offices and work-shops in new and exciting roles.

Whereas the main differences between a main-frame and a mini are size, power and cost, the micro is of an essentially different breed. The larger computers incorporate many micro-processors with several of them grouped together to carry out some of the operations. In a micro, on the other hand, a single micro-processor will be responsible for one or more functions. Necessarily, then, a micro cannot be as powerful as a mini and this has to be weighed against its advantages of very low cost, flexibility, portability and ability of the user to control and manage it himself.

The first generation of micros were built around silicon chips that operate with 8-bit (one byte) words. The previous section described how a word-size of 16 bits (two bytes) was suitable for small computers and further clever computing algorithms are needed to permit an 8-bit computer to operate satisfactorily. These algorithms are built into the computer's controlling device known as its *operating system* and as many man-years go into the development of the operating system as go into the design of the electronic machinery (the 'hardware'). The importance of the operating system will be re-emphasized in the next section.

Types of micro-computer

INTRODUCTION

Micro-computers come in all shapes, sizes and description. The majority are single-user (that is only one person can use them at a time) and for that reason are sometimes termed 'personal' computers. This can be misleading when applied to business machines but it is useful to describe the small micros sold for home use.

Before describing some of the different types of micro-computer it will be useful to explain some of the terminology commonly used in computing. When computers are said to have 1,000 bytes of storage memory, they really have 1,024 bytes, which is 2 to the power 10 (remembering that everything to do with computers relates to binary representations). Hence, 64,000 is actually 65,536 (2 to the power 16) but is written 64K, ie 64

16

Kilobytes. This will refer to the storage (ie the number of pigeon holes) available to the user for his programs and data and, since the user must be able to address these locations at will, it is called 'random access memory' or RAM for short.

Another part of storage is put aside for the manufacturer to keep the control programs and programs that translate user-written computer commands into patterns of 1's and 0's that form the computer's machine language. This part of storage is strictly not for the user and is therefore 'read only memory' or ROM for short.

HOBBY COMPUTERS

Scores of families now have a micro in their home. Their uses range from computer games, through education to basic home accounting. Their attraction is incomprehensible to many people but there is no doubt that they can give a great deal of pleasure to their owners. Prices start at under £50 for a fully fledged, though limited, micro with 1,000 bytes of storage, ie 1,000 locations to store the program and data. This may sound considerable but each character in a program command, such as 'LET X = Y + Z' uses one of these locations. Consequently, the size of the programs is quite limited. However, boxes containing more storage (typically 16,000 bytes) can be bought, together with literally thousands of ready written programs. Visual display is usually via an ordinary home television set and programs can be stored on a cassette tape recorder. A cheap printer can be bought to complete a remarkably low cost 'starter' computer kit.

Users who wish to take their computing more seriously or who want better games facilities and colour display have to pay more but can still buy a machine with up to 32,000 or even 64,000 bytes of storage for under £400.

BUSINESS COMPUTERS

Some of the more sophisticated machines sold primarily as hobby computers can also be used in a commercial environment. However, they have the one fundamental disadvantage that, without the addition of further equipment, they can only store

17

programs for reuse on cassette tape. Reading programs back into the computer from cassette is a slow process and, since everything is stored sequentially, it can be frustrating trying to locate a program stored at the end of the tape. A much more efficient medium for external storage is a disc which is a device resembling a gramophone record. Programs and data can be retrieved rapidly from any part of the disc and they are capable of storing many more bytes. Once a disc unit is added, the price rises to over £500 and the user will be looking for a greater return for his investment. It is more or less essential to have the facility for two discs, to enable back-up copies of programs and data to be made, and so a basic micro will comprise:

central processing unit (plus internal storage – CPU)

visual display unit – VDU (of greater clarity than a home television)

disc unit with facility for 2 discs

printer.

Most of these basic models will come in a complete package (except for the printer) with prices starting at under £1,500. Figure 7 on page 19 is a typical example.

Other computers will be sold with either the visual display unit or the disc unit, or both, in a separate box. A few models have an integral printer, some of which close up like suitcases to be carried around, complete from site to site. There are also 'hand held' varieties but they usually have a cassette tape instead of a disc unit.

As important as the computer and the associated equipment (the *hardware*) is the *software* available on any given computer. Program 'packages' are written to work under a particular operating system and it is essential to make the correct choice. Unlike main-frames and minis which each work on a different operating system, many 8-bit business micros work under an operating system called CP/M (short for 'control processor for micro-computers'). The advantage of this is that there is a vast portfolio of packages available for most 8-bit micros.

Some popular micros, such as those with the Apple, Commodore and Tandy labels, have their own operating systems and because of their popularity many programs have been written

18

Figure 7
A small business computer (Apple IIe)
(Courtesy MBS Personal Computers)

specifically for these makes. Even so, they can usually be adapted to work under the CP/M operating system. One of the factors affecting the speed of operation within a computer is the amount of data that can be processed in one go. As the name implies, 8-bit micros deal with one byte at a time. Manufacturers are now offering machines that perform operations two bytes at a time. Thus, there are 16-bit (two bytes) or, if only some operations are carried out this way, 'pseudo' 16-bit micros which are available. The difference between the operation of these machines can be likened to different types of roads. An 8-bit (one byte) computer is equivalent to a single carriageway road; a 16-bit (two bytes) computer is equivalent to a dual carriageway. A pseudo 16-bit machine resembles a road which is a mixture of both single and dual carriageways. There are even some that are 32-bit, and some that are a cross between 16-bit and 32-bit, machines. In general, the more bits there are the more powerful the machine. (This is not a reflection of the number of components but the amount of data being processed at one time!) However, hardware designers

19

and engineers are months, if not years ahead of the program writers – the reverse of Babbage's experience. Consequently, the software available for the new 16-bit and 32-bit machines is not yet as plentiful as for the 8-bit micros. Two operating systems are widely used on the 16-bit micros – CP/M-86 and MS-DOS. Some micro manufacturers have hedged their bets and offer both CP/M-86 and MS-DOS but the decision of IBM to concentrate on MS-DOS for their desk-top computer means that software will be available more quickly for that option.

Some micro-computers have two CPU micro-processor chips, one for running 8-bit software and one for running 16-bit software. Figure 8 on page 21 shows one of these machines.

MULTI-USER MICROS AND NETWORKING

Many users of business micros will be happy to have a computer for his or her own personal use or, at least, for use by one person at a time. But there are many applications, in personnel administration for example, where it will be necessary for two or more people to use the programs and data. For these situations, a 'multi-user' micro is required. These come in two types:

1   two or more VDUs attached to a central box that is partitioned into two or more CPUs (controlled by a shared operating system) plus a disc storage unit (see figure 9 on page 22).

2   individual combined VDU and CPUs that share a common disc storage unit (see figure 10 on page 22).

In the latter case, it is usually possible for a disc unit to be attached to the remote VDU and CPU devices, thus giving each user a self-contained computer but with the ability to access a central disc storage unit when necessary.

Multi-user machines like those described above require special operating systems to cope with the fact that several users have to be serviced (apparently) simultaneously. The multi-user versions of CP/M and CP/M86 are called MP/M and MP/M86; the (pseudo) 32-bit micros have a variety of operating systems available to them but one of the most powerful is UNIX which was originally developed for mini-computers.

Another way in which more than one user can access a common store of programs and data is by means of a technique called

Figure 8
A dual processor micro-computer (DEC Rainbow)
(Courtesy MBS Personal Computers)

networking. In these systems, each user has his own single-user micro that can communicate with either any other micro in the network or a shared facility such as a disc or a printer.

There are three types of networks: star, which is similar to a multi-user computer; ring, where several computers and facilities (disc units, printers) are joined to each other by wiring; linear, similar to a ring except that each unit is attached to a central 'highway'. There will be a maximum number of devices per network but, by using a node of the network as either a new central hub (in the case of a ring) or as a link to another network (or extension of the current network) the number of devices can be greatly increased.

A system of networked micros can be a cost-effective way of replicating the power of a mini-computer. Not only are the extensive facilities of a mini available, but the user also has his own independent secure computer sitting in his office. The barrier to the speedy introduction of networking has been the lack of a universal standard system. However, several major firms have

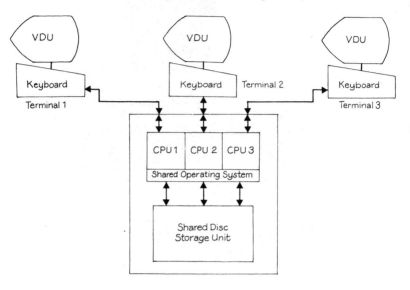

Figure 9
Multi-user system (star arrangement)

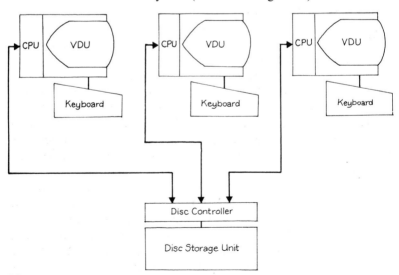

Figure 10
Multi-user system (branch arrangement)

invested a great deal of research and money into developing and supporting network systems.

Computer equipment

In many cases, the user will be buying a complete package of main box, screen and keyboard, printer and disc unit but each element is an entity and it is important that each satisfies the user. The main component of the computer, containing the control, arithmetic logic unit and internal storage (memory) is, for most buyers a black box.

VISUAL DISPLAY UNITS (VDUs) AND KEYBOARDS

The most visible part of the micro is the display screen and poor design can make using the computer a strain. The screen will be attached to a keyboard and the total package must be carefully evaluated.

The common size for a monitor screen is 12″, measured across a diagonal. Some are larger (15″ for example) and consequently are easier on the eye. Some portable computers have screens that are smaller, but these usually have the facility for a larger monitor to be plugged in.

The second important design point is the colour of the screen, background and typed characters. Most offer different shades of green whereas others have printing on a dark grey background or shades of orange. The standard number of character positions is 80 across the screen (ie 80 columns) with approximately 24 lines of print. Some systems use one or more lines (rows) at the bottom of the screen to display some information such as a menu of standard functions. The sharpness of the character images is a function of the number of dots, grouped together in blocks called 'pixels' that are used for each character position. Thus a screen with 80,000 pixels will have sharper images (ie greater resolution) than one with 40,000 pixels.

Keyboards are either fixed to the screen or, more usually these days, joined by a flexible cord. All have the basic array of keys, with the letters of the alphabet arranged as on a typewriter and a row of numbers above them. These are usually known as QWERTY keyboards after the first six letters on the top row of keys (see figure 11 below).

The next step up will be the incorporation of a numeric keypad arranged like that on a calculator. Other keys that can be added are called 'function keys', labelled F1, F2 ... and these can be programmed to save the user having to type long instructions repeatedly. Similarly, some keyboards have keys dedicated to word processing facilities, such as 'move block' etc.

Figure 11
Basic keyboard

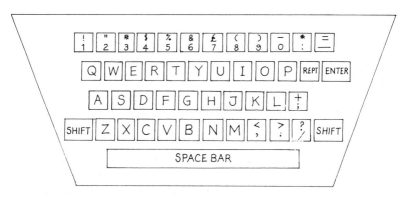

The depth of keystroke is another aspect of design that can be important to the user. As with other features of the VDU and keyboard, the user must always feel comfortable when sitting down to work at the computer. Chapter 4 describes how data can be entered via a VDU and consequently displayed for examination. This will involve letters and numbers being shown in highlight against a dark background. Some VDUs have an option for reversing the display so that the foreground is dark and the background light. This is known as 'inverse video'.

The position on the screen which is currently active, ie showing the piece of data being acted upon is pinpointed by a spot of light (sometimes flashing to attract attention) called a 'cursor'.

A more dramatic, and sometimes more informative, way of

24

presenting results is by means of a graphical display. In many cases, however, these displays are more decorative than useful but there are occasions, such as investigation of trends, when a graph can give more information than a set of numbers. Where necessary, a full colour monitor can be purchased.

PRINTERS

The simplest type of printer for business micros uses a matrix of dots to build up a printed character. The more dots there are in the matrix, the better the definition, but some give improved quality by over printing, shifting the position of the dots slightly to partially fill in the gaps. Very expensive versions will overprint four times, each time slightly offset, so that the print will appear to be fully joined up. A simple dot-matrix printer will suffice for most internal office purposes.

Speeds vary from 80 characters per second (cps) to over 200 cps (about a minute per A4 page) bearing in mind that the actual rated typing speed is not achieved because the print head has to return to the left hand side of the platen and the paper has to move up for the next line to be printed.

For external correspondence, important internal reports and other word processing applications a dot-matrix printer will not be satisfactory. Typewriter quality is provided by 'daisy-wheel' printers, so called because the typewriter hammer system is replaced by a rotating wheel (see figure 12 on page 26). An alternative to the daisy wheel is provided by a 'thimble' which resembles a cut-off golf ball. Daisy wheels and thimbles are interchangeable so that the user can keep a stock of print faces and special characters.

Continuous paper feed is effected by sprockets at the sides of the printing platen but provision is made for the automatic friction feeding of single sheets of paper (A4 for example) for the typing of letters or reports.

Speeds of daisywheel printers are in the range of 15cps to 75cps, much slower than the dot-matrix variety. For some applications, especially in the personnel area, it can be advantageous to have both types of printer.

The following is a checklist of facilities:

Figure 12
Daisy wheel

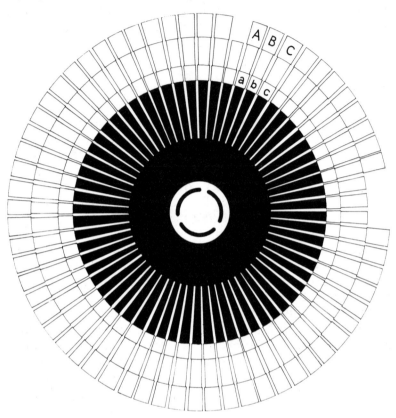

True descenders (dot matrix printers)	do the letters g, y etc print above and below the line?
Underlining	will this be true underlining or will an extra line be taken up?
Bold type	will the printer overprint?
Proportional spacing	important for proper word processing use.

Number of print positions	some cheaper printers have only 80 print positions; others have the option to compress characters to print up to 120/132 or 160 characters.
Number of copies	this ranges from 1 to over 5; the more copies there are, the heavier the paper and a special table/feeder tray may be necessary to stop the paper slipping.
Serial/parallel printers	most printers used for micros work in serial mode, ie one bit is transmitted at a time from the computer to the printer. This is slower than parallel operation which allows the concurrent transmission of more than one bit, but is a considerably cheaper technology.
Attached keyboard	Some daisy wheel printers have the option of being disconnected from the computer to work as an ordinary typewriter.
Intelligence	Some computers store a line of print in advance so that they can print as the carriage is returning – this is called bi-directional printing.
Graphics/colour output	good quality dot matrix printers are capable of producing graphical output but colour-printing is performed by specialist devices. Prices for colour plotters are in the same range as daisy wheel printers but for most personnel applications, they are a slow and expensive 'optional extra'.

Cassette tapes store information, programs, songs etc. in sequential order, as shown in figure 13 below. Thus, finding a particular set of data, or a program, and reading it off are slow operations. A disc unit works much more quickly. A thin magnetized plastic disc with many hundreds of 'grooves' etched on it revolves at high speed within a paper sleeve (see figure 14 on page 29). An electronic pick-up arm moves back and forward across a 'window' and the disc control unit (also called the disc operating system, or DOS) instructs it to read 'data bits' as their location flashes past the window. Since the disc operating system will have access to an index of where everything is stored, access speeds can be very fast.

Floppy discs (or diskettes) come in three standard sizes, 3.5″, 5.25″ and 8″ diameters. The most common is 5.25″ but, unfortunately, there are no standards for their manufacture or their disk operating system and so it is usually impossible to take a 5.25″ disc out of one machine and insert it for use in another make. However, since IBM entered the micro-computer market, and are expected to capture a significant portion of that market, some other manufacturers have begun to provide 5.25″ disc units that are compatible with those of IBM. There is an international standard for 8″ floppy discs but only a few manufacturers offer this size as an option on their micros. For a payroll application

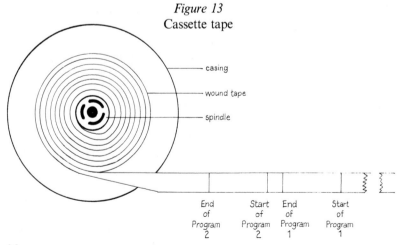

Figure 13
Cassette tape

casing

wound tape

spindle

End
of
Program
2

Start
of
Program
2

End
of
Program
1

Start
of
Program
1

Figure 14
Floppy disc

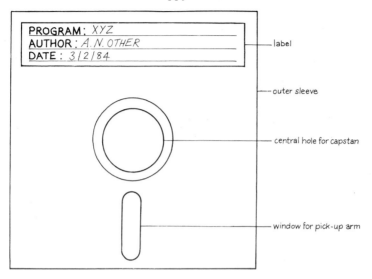

where it is required to use the Banks Automatic Clearing Service (BACS) for the automatic updating of employees' bank accounts, 8″ discs are mandatory, except where a 'dial up' operation is offered.

The recent development of 3.5″ floppy discs is interesting since they are supplied in more solid packages and should therefore be more robust. Although few micros support this size at the moment, it is hoped that the computer industry will establish a standard for it.

The packing of data on floppy discs can be either single density (SD) or double density (DD), ie twice as much information stored on the disc. Some devices will also make use of both sides of the disc and in this way up to four times the amount of data can be stored. Floppy disc capacities range from 300,000 (300k) bytes up to one million bytes (1mb) or even more. This sounds considerable but in personnel work it is often the case that more than one disc will be required to store the set of programs or files of personnel data. A floppy disc based computer can be used but it can become quite tedious swopping discs in and out as required. For most personnel work, especially where payroll is also included, a large storage device is required. For micros this is provided by a sealed disc unit containing one disc, or several discs stacked one on top of the other and made of more solid material than the flexible transportable floppy discs. These 'hard' disc units can store from 3mb to over 80mb and since multiple pick-up heads are used several pieces of data can be accessed simultaneously. Consequently a computer with this type of storage, called a hard disc (or Winchester after the IBM research project that developed them) will work several times faster than a floppy disc based system. Hard disc units can usually be added to most computers but it is often very much cheaper to buy a system with one included in its original configuration.

The portability of floppy discs make them ideal for keeping security copies of programs and data. Consequently a computer with a hard disc unit will also have a floppy disc unit so that the contents of the hard disc can be copied and stored in a safe place. A 20mb hard disc will fill over 20 floppy discs if it is to be fully 'backed-up' and this operation can take three or four minutes per floppy disc. To reduce this time, it will be sensible to make two or three security copies of the programs when they are first installed and then regularly back-up the file of data only.

A faster method of taking a back-up of data that is held on a hard disc is by means of a cartridge tape, a special type of magnetic tape capable of holding many millions of bytes of data. The price of these has been reduced considerably so that they are worth considering as a time-saving alternative to using multiple floppy discs. The recent development of a removable hard disc provides an alternative high volume back-up storage medium.

Communications

Many large companies have personnel departments in several locations and it will be desirable for the remote office to be linked into the computer system. There are several ways in which this can be effected but each will require specialized equipment to convert the digital electronically stored data in the computer or terminal into electrical impulses that can be carried by cable over long distances. These converters are called modulators/de-modulators, or modems for short. The simplest modem is the 'acoustic coupler' which converts computer data into sound waves for direct input to a telephone set. The data then travels down the telephone system to a receiver at the other end and another acoustic coupler decodes it for the remote computer or terminal. Data travels slowly (30 characters per second) by this method but the equipment costs only about £200.

More expensive modems (£500 and upwards) can provide faster transmission down the telephone network and for most personnel applications this will be quite adequate. Some companies will have their own transmission lines independent of the public telephone network. These lines will often consist of clusters of lines offering high speed transmission which are not subject to the line noise that is sometimes present on telephone lines.

These multiple line systems require special modems called 'multi-plexors' that aggregate and disaggregate the signals for the several users or devices at each end of the lines. This can also be used to serve a remote user with more than one device, such as a VDU and a printer.

There will be occasions when it will be necessary to link the micro to either another micro or a mini or main-frame computer. Linking to another micro requires each computer to have a software package loaded (the same package on each micro!) and a cable that is specially wired to the specifications of the particular micros concerned. Linking to a mini or main frame requires a program to be loaded on the micro which enables the micro to pretend that it is a terminal of the host machine. These software packages are readily available and not very expensive but, as with the wiring of links between micros, they may require specialist professional advice.

Graphics

On page 25 it was stated that there are few occasions when graphical displays or outputs are necessary. However, if the decision has been made to have graphical capabilities, the type of display and the necessary equipment will have to be chosen. In personnel use, the most common graphical displays are:

graphs (lines drawn on a scale grid)

bar charts (blocks whose size represents numerical values)

pie charts (shapes with slices cut out to represent different percentages)

organization charts.

Both graphs and bar charts can be drawn on standard screens and printers. Most computers, with the appropriate VDUs can provide colour visual displays, including pie charts. Colour printed output will require special programs and printing devices.

Buying a micro system

Choosing a micro-computer system can be a confusing and frustrating process. The case studies in chapters 5 and 6 describe how two companies approached the problem and the factors that determined their final choice. However, there are some basic rules that can be stated for general guidance.

RULE 1: DECIDE WHAT THE SYSTEM IS TO BE USED FOR

This may seem to be a very obvious first step but it is vital for the administrator to be clear in his mind exactly why it has been decided to buy a computer. There will be many distractions on the road to the final choice and so the primary purpose of the system must be always borne in mind.

RULE 2: CHOOSE THE SOFTWARE FIRST AND THEN THE HARDWARE

Developments in hardware technology guarantee that almost any facility that is required will be possible. However, finding a program that provides all the chosen facilities is much more difficult. Compromises may have to be made as a last resort but eventually it should be possible to find a program to satisfy most of the identified requirements. The program may be an 'off-the-shelf' package or it may be a package that has been 'customized' to the buyer's requirements.

RULE 3: RESEARCH THE MARKET

Computer magazines will carry advertisements for both hardware and software and reading a few of these publications is a good starting point. There will be many software products mentioned for payroll and one or two for personnel record keeping. It will not be clear which combination of hardware and software is appropriate for a particular organization and the personnel officer will have to read about the subject in some detail. Other reference works of interest include the IDS *Survey of personnel/payroll systems* and articles in the *IPM Digest* and *Personnel Managment.*

The potential buyer will need help and at some point it will be necessary to seek independent advice. There are three main sources of this advice:

1   from within the organization
2   from outside consultants
3   from personnel departments in other companies.

The obvious place to visit within the organization is the data processing department. They will have a wealth of experience in computing and will help in preparing a checklist of requirements. However, their knowledge may be confined to minis and mainframes and it may also be related to the products of a particular manufacture. It is essential not to be swayed towards buying a computer that is either bigger than necessary or is not really suitable for the purpose intended.

Outside consultancy advice should be unbiased and will shorten the search process considerably. It will, however, cost money and if this route is chosen it is advisable for the user/client to draw up a closely defined brief for a fixed cost feasibility study. The report resulting from this study should offer alternative listing the costs, advantages and disadvantages of each.

Computer salesmen will proclaim the virtues of their particular systems but the best people to talk to are the actual users of the systems of interest. Most users will be quite willing to discuss their experiences with the systems they have installed. Much can be learnt this way and a useful list of good points and pitfalls can be drawn up.

RULE 4: CONSIDER FUTURE REQUIREMENTS

Before the final decision can be made it is necessary to review all the basic requirements and estimate whether future developments will make the system inadequate. Particular points to bear in mind are:

1 number of simultaneous users

2 storage capacity.

Not all computers are capable of supporting more than one VDU and, unless it is absolutely certain that a single-user system will suffice for the foreseeable future, it is recommended that a multi-user computer (or one that is capable of up-grading to multi-use) be bought.

The inconvenience of continually swopping floppy discs in and out of the disc drive has already been mentioned. Hence, it is recommended that a hard disc be included in the hardware configuration. The extra cost of additional capacity on a hard disc is very small, sometimes as little as £200 per 5mb, and so it would be foolish to skimp on the size of disc.

Maintenance and support

A new computer will come with a 90-day (or in some cases a 1-year) warranty. Should it go wrong within that period, the owner will probably have to return the machine to the supplier for repair or replacement. After that, it is advisable to take out a contract with a specialist maintenance company who will undertake to visit the installation and repair the fault in situ. Some contracts may include a maximum attendance time which can range between four hours and 48 hours. Micros are generally sold through agents, sometimes shopkeepers, who in turn buy them from wholesalers (called distributors), who will also be the importers if the product is foreign. Some distributors offer a maintenance service but by no means most. The buyer must then choose a maintenance company that offers the service required. For installations outside the main conurbations, it is important to check that a service engineer is based locally and can satisfy the contractual arrangements concerning response time.

Hardware maintenance costs are usually in the range of 12

per cent to 17 per cent per annum of the total buying price. The contractor will provide regular service inspections as well as repair facilities. For VDUs and printers an alternative is to take out a 'parts insurance' contract with a broker, but this is not recommended for the main computer box.

Examples of micro-computer systems

The list of micro-computer configurations given in figure 15 on page 36 is by no means comprehensive but has been designed to provide a guide to the various types of computer available. The potential buyer is reminded to choose a software package or customized product first and then choose a computer. It should also be noted that the price guide does not include provision for a printer and its attendant equipment, such as acoustic hood and stand, but it does include the cost of the VDU(s).

Costs and cost effectiveness

The basic cost of any micro-computer system is only the starting point in considering whether the investment will be money well spent. The annual cost of maintaining the computer hardware and keeping the software up to date must be added. The maintenance of software is particularly important when the system includes items which are subject to legislative requirements such as statutory sick pay.

The cost of using the system should be taken into account. Considerable quantities of paper and other consumables such as printer ribbons and floppy discs may be used. In particular, the costs of connecting other locations to a central computer using either public or leased telephone lines can be substantial. Loading and updating the information which is used by the system can incur considerable staff cost. A computerized personnel records system is of no value until the data has been entered. It may be possible to load basic information electronically, using records produced by the computerized payroll system, for example. However, information will usually have to be entered using the

Figure 15
Examples of micro-computer configurations

Type of Computer	Number of Users	CPU Capacity	Floppy disc		Hard Disc Capacity	Operating System	Price Guide £
			Size	Capacity			
8-bit (floppy disc)	1	64K	5.25″	350K	—	CP/M	2300–2700
8-bit (hard disc)	1	64K	5.25″	350K	5mb	CP/M	3000–3500
16-bit (floppy disc)	1	128K	5.25″	760K	—	MS-DOS	2000–2300
16-bit (hard disc)	1	128K	5.25″	760K	20mb	MS-DOS	3500–4000
8-bit (multi-user)	3	208K	8″	556K	10mb	MP/M	9000–9500
32-bit (multi-user)	8	512K	8″	556K	20mb	UNIX	18500–19000

keyboard and VDU screen. The staff who load the information will work from existing records if available and exercises will have to be carried out to establish any missing items of information and to verify the data once it has been loaded, to ensure that no mistakes have been made. This process involves many man-hours of work; either staff will be taken away from their normal duties or temporary staff will have to be employed. A schedule to load data 'as and when time allows' is unlikely to be successful.

Personnel administrators are frequently expected to cost-justify the installation of a computerized system. Unless staff savings are achieved it is very difficult to carry out such a justification because a monetary value cannot easily be put on the benefits of the system. On the other hand, computerized personnel recording should improve administration and provide better management information. In addition, it can improve job satisfaction in the personnel department and release staff from routine record keeping duties in order to concentrate on other important work.

The comments made by a personnel assistant in the company which is the subject of the case study described in chapter 5 illustrates this point. In this instance the personnel assistant had been relieved of the manual updating of basic record cards, summary sheets and the calculation of manpower statistics. This record keeping chore was reduced to entering information to the computerized system; listings and analyses were then produced automatically. The introduction of the micro-computer based record system was viewed very favourably by the personnel assistant because it had enabled him to be employed on other, more interesting and more important duties.

3 :: Systems available on micro-computers

Introduction

In an ideal world, personnel administrators would have access to the 'perfect' or 'total' computerized system. This system would be so comprehensive and easy to use that staff levels within the personnel department would be kept to an absolute minimum and the administrator's work load would be so reduced that he would have ample time to sit back and plan manpower strategies, recruitment campaigns, training policies and all the other creative tasks.

Maybe this would not really be an ideal world and, in any case, it is not attainable. To achieve anything like a 'perfect' system would require a huge investment in program development time, particularly as the system would have to be readily adaptable to the special requirements of different organizations. Some systems available on large main-frame computers try to achieve perfection. They do not succeed, of course, and it is therefore important to stress that systems available on micro-computers, necessarily less powerful than those on mainframes, cannot hope to satisfy all of any individual's requirements.

All computerized personnel systems either utilize or adapt generalized database packages or are built around a new, more specialized, database system. Thus, it will be useful to define the concepts of databases before describing the types of personnel package that are available.

Databases

Definitions of a database range from:

nothing more than a computer-base record keeping system

to

collection of stored operational data used by the application systems of some particular enterprise
(*source* Date CJ, *An Introduction to Database Systems.* Addison-Wesley, 1981)

The latter definition is somewhat daunting but it does contain the essential elements necessary to describe the structure and workings of a database.

First, the 'enterprise' may be a company, a government organization or a personnel department. Secondly, an application system may concern stock recording, medical primary prognosis or a payroll. The third element, operational data, covers not only the actual data to be stored but also the inter-relationships that bind the various pieces of information together.

As an example, consider a list of executives in a company that operates in several locations (see figure 16 below).

Figure 16
Sample data

Employee number	Surname	Status	Location
1	Baldwin	2	London
2	Davidson	1	Manchester
3	Adams	3	Manchester
4	Evans	2	Glasgow
5	Clark	3	Belfast

If there were only five such employees then this table would be an adequately efficient method of recording the data. However, if there were many employees to be kept track of then a separate location file might be needed (see figure 17 on page 40).

Figure 17
Separation of data files

Employee file			Location pointer	Location file
Employee number	Surname	Status		Location
1	Baldwin	2		Belfast
2	Davidson	1		
3	Adams	3		Glasgow
4	Evans	2		London
5	Clark	3		Manchester

This process can be continued so that in this simple example there might be a master employee file, with employee number and surname, that has pointers to status and location files.

The relationships between the various data files have to be fully described in the setting up of the database. The initial operation and all the storing and retrieval functions are controlled by the 'data base management system' or DBMS. The whole operation is shown schematically in figure 18 opposite.

Multi-purpose database systems, by their very nature, have to be designed to allow for any file inter-relationships that might be required. Their efficiency can be measured by the size of the database that can be accommodated linked with the speed at which data can be added or retrieved. The same criteria obviously apply to databases designed for specific applications but these have the advantage of having structures suitable for those applications. Naturally, the larger the computer the larger the database system that it can support. The very large software systems are available for purchase from between £20,000 and £50,000 or are offered by computer bureaux on a time and licence arrangement. Mini-computer systems cost from £2,000 to £20,000 and, whilst offering similar facilities to those on main-frames will be slower because of the speed of the computers themselves.

40

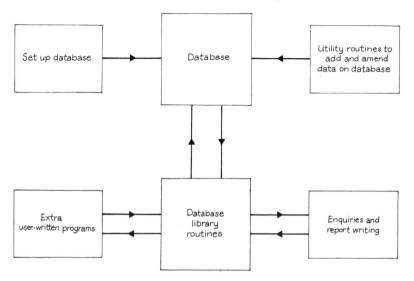

Figure 18
Schematic diagram of database operations

Personnel database systems

Specialized personnel systems that are available on main-frames and mini-computers can offer the full facilities of the large generalized database systems together with features of specific interest to personnel administrators. Many of these features will also be available on micro-based systems but these are smaller and slower and their programs cannot match those on minis and main-frames for power and comprehension. Again, it is a question of balancing the range of facilities against the cost and usefulness.

There are many aspects to personnel management and figure 19 on page 42 shows how these refer back to the database of personnel details. Some systems concentrate on the pure record keeping and reporting activities. These can reduce the manual effort required within the personnel department significantly but take only limited advantage of the opportunities afforded by a computerized database.

A second approach is to access the database by a set of programs, each one of the set serving one aspect of the personnel function. Figure 20 on page 42 shows how this can work.

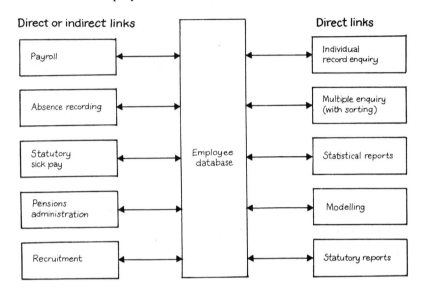

Figure 19
Employee database and associated activities

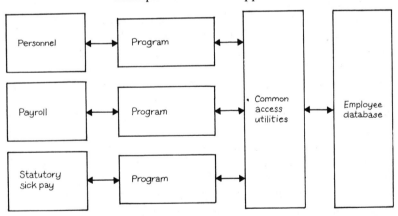

Figure 20
Example of Modular Approach

An advantage of the modular approach is that the user can build up his system gradually, familiarizing himself with one set of procedures before installing the next.

A third approach is to have an integrated system that has one interface program between the user and database but caters for

42

different administrative requirements. A 'complete' system would cover everything set out in figure 19 but it is unlikely that a micro could support such a system.

Personnel record keeping

Most organizations using micros in personnel administration will use the computer chiefly for maintaining their personnel records. This application makes use of the machine's ability to *store* and *retrieve* information.

The use of a computer system to store information is analogous to a card index. Basic information about each employee, such as home address, salary or wage, job title and national insurance number is stored on each employee's record. A micro-computer system stores this electronically on a floppy or hard disc rather than on a piece of card kept in a filing tray. When *storing* data the computer's advantage is that a very large number of records may be kept on a single disc.

The computer based personnel records system also has advantages when *retrieving* information. Computer based systems, like the card index, can quickly locate an individual's record. The information will be displayed on a VDU or a printed copy will be produced. Such systems are also very quick to identify which records meet some specified criteria. For instance, it may be necessary for manpower planning to identify the number of skilled operatives who will retire in the next 10 years. The system should be capable of examining each record and counting the number of employees falling into that category. Similarly, the system should enable the personnel executive engaged in recruitment to identify potential candidates already employed by the organization and to examine their records in turn. For instance the records of all accountants over the age of 25 but under the age of 40, earning less than £15,000 might be selected.

These types of basic enquiry are typical of the use made of micro-computer based personnel record keeping systems. The micro-computer's value comes not only from being a convenient method of storing information but also from the system's ability to quickly retrieve particular records according to specified parameters. One example of this type of operation occurred in one of the companies included in the case studies. This was the apparently simple problem of identifying the number of staff with two or more years service who would qualify for a share option scheme. Before the company computerized its records, the existing manual records were distributed around the operating units. The central personnel department had to request each location's personnel department to identify those with the relevant service. The records in each location were then individually examined and a count taken. The final result was sent back to the central office where the figures were consolidated. This exercise took at least one week, whereas a similar exercise undertaken after the computer had been installed was completed in one hour.

Reference has already been made to the advantages of integrated systems. A great deal, although not all, of the information used by personnel records systems will also be required by the payroll. However, payroll is seen as an accounting function by many organizations. In addition, many internal and external auditors prefer to separate the payroll and personnel systems so that checks and balances can be built into the payroll to improve the internal controls.

The organizational and control reasons outlined above have led many companies to develop separate payroll and personnel systems. Payroll was one of the earliest functions to be computerized using main-frame computers and many organizations have a computerized payroll based on their main-frame computer as well as holding manual personnel records. Perhaps surprisingly such organizations will consider the use of independent micro-computer systems for personnel record keeping. There are apparently two main reasons for such a decision. First, many main-frame data processing departments are unable to provide an appropriate system. Secondly, many organizations require a system which is independent of the main-frame. This second point has been recognized as an important component in data protection agreements by at least one trade union.

The interaction of the payroll system and the micro-computer based personnel system must be carefully considered, particularly where a main-frame computer is used for the payroll.

Clearly there are savings in time and effort which can be achieved when a micro-computer based personnel system is installed in addition to a 'main-frame' if data has to be entered to only one of the systems. Information, such as salary details, are then transferred electronically to the other system. Chapter two refers to the possibility of linking a micro-computer to a main-frame and such facilities for communication are available for many types of computer.

Absence recording and statutory sick pay

In many companies the introduction of statutory sick pay (SSP) will have highlighted the interaction between payroll and personnel systems. For SSP purposes, records have to be kept detailing days of sickness absence. Calculations of SSP have to be carried out on the basis of this information, taking into account the period of incapacity for work, qualifying days, waiting days and linked periods of incapacity for work. Records are also required to comply with the rules relating to exclusions and transfers.

In certain organizations the limit of the payroll department's involvement in SSP has been to accept the amount of SSP to be paid from an outside source and to recover the appropriate amount from National Insurance contributions. Other payrolls are able to take the dates of absence and complete the SSP calculations.

Some personnel departments have extended the administration set up to deal with SSP to provide an absence control system. Micro-computer based software has proved powerful in this field. One such system not only meets all the statutory requirements of the SSP legislation but also provides a facility for maintaining absence records using different categories of absence as follows:

sickness

unauthorized absence

paid holidays

other paid leave

time off for trade union and public duties

compassionate leave

time off for education and training

medical leave.

A facility for the user to specify two of their own categories, such as territorial army leave, is also provided.

To assist the personnel department to control employee absence, the system can analyse the data entered and produce a number of reports. It is also sophisticated enough to cater for companies that have different accounting years for holidays, company sickness benefit and SSP. For example, to compare the sickness absence records of particular departments the system can calculate the total days lost and the percentage of lost time in each department and in the organization as a whole. The absence records of individual employees can be examined using a matrix showing daily absence over a 52 week period. This provides a simple way of identifying absence patterns, showing, for example, that a certain employee is generally absent on Fridays.

A system such as this, set up to meet statutory requirements and which is required to service the payroll, becomes a powerful tool for the personnel manager.

Integrated systems

The personnel record keeping, statutory sick pay (SSP) and other functions can each be serviced by 'stand alone' programs or by programs that share common database facilities, ie the modular approach. However, there are good reasons for integrating as many functions as is feasible into a single combined program.

Both the modular and integrated systems benefit from the advantages of keeping a single database. Among the benefits are:

reduction of duplicated data; this is particularly true when the payroll and personnel functions share the comprehensive employee database since in separate systems so much data is recorded and stored twice.

consistency of the data; this is attained because each item of data is input only once and is stored in a single location.

maintenance of security; a single enforceable security system can be imposed to cover all access to the data held on file.

integrity of the data; it is easier to keep the data accurate if it is stored in a single set of files.

The advantages of a single database can be similarly applied to a single (ie integrated) program system. There can be some overhead cost, in terms of slower program running speeds, from an integrated program but if it has been well designed this can be kept to an acceptable minimum. There is an additional advantage in that using an integrated system means that the user need learn to operate only one program.

The simplest form of integration is to incorporate SSP recording and calculating into the payroll suite. This is an obvious step since SSP has ramifications both in the make-up of an employee's payslip and in the content of the financial reports and National Insurance returns. Similarly SSP is linked to absence recording and the company sickpay system and so it may find a home in the general personnel management system.

The obvious next step is to integrate all three elements of personnel record keeping, SSP and payroll. Figure 21 shows an outline of such a system. The various files are separated out for clarity although they will in practice be less sharply delineated.

Although the system may itself be integrated there may be a need to have selective access to sections of the data for reasons of security or confidentiality. For example, some users may have the

Figure 21
Outline of an integrated personnel/SSP/payroll system

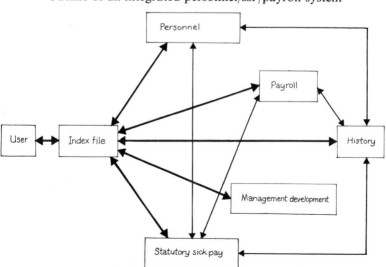

authority to view and amend personnel details such as address or medical information but have no equivalent authority with regards to payroll data. Access to the data will be via a visual display unit (VDU) and the whole question of how the data can be input, viewed and amended will be more fully dealt with in chapter 4.

Extensions to integrated systems

If the company introducing the personnel system employs people who are paid an hourly rate, the raw data for the payroll will usually be held on clock cards. A clock card administrator will transcribe the data on to computer input forms which will then be given to the data processing or payroll department for the data to be finally keyed into the computer. However, it is now possible to bypass all these stages. There are electronic time clocks on the market with built-in microprocessor chips that can store the data in such a manner that it can be accessed directly by a micro-computer. Figure 22 below shows the outline of such a system.

Figure 22
Outline of an automatic clock card recording system

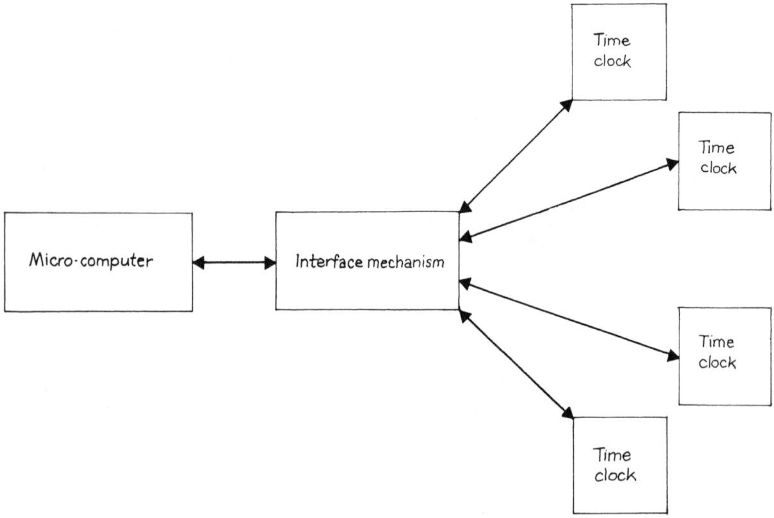

The time clocks are accessed once a week to draw off the hours worked, by pay rate, for each employee. The micro-based payroll system then calculates the weekly pay and productivity bonus, if applicable. An additional advantage of such a system is that the time clocks can be interrogated at any time to see who is absent, who has been late and also to keep a track of labour mobility if that is wanted by the organization.

The integration of clock card recording with the payroll/personnel/SSP system gives the personnel (or personnel/payroll) manager a fairly complete coverage of the administrative functions within his compass. The missing module is pensions administration. In many organizations there is a separate pensions department, usually reporting to a pensions fund manager. For this reason, and also because of the specialist nature of the work, pension fund administration is not normally integrated with other aspects of personnel work.

Naturally, there must be some links between the payroll and pensions functions because pension contributions have to be notified and cumulative payments and National Insurance contributions have also to be reported, either annually or when an employee leaves. Similarly, either the personnel or payroll departments have to keep the pensions department informed of all staff movements or changes in employees' circumstances that affect pension entitlements.

Micro-based pension administration systems are not numerous and those that have been developed have not made much impact in the market place. Hence, the links between personnel/payroll and pensions have been via paper memoranda and computer printed output. This will gradually change as program writers solve the problems presented when trying to cope with the volume and complexity of pension fund data and procedure on a micro-computer.

Another example of how a micro based personnel system can be linked to another aspect of personnel administration concerns the practice of running the payroll either on the organization's own mainframe or at a computer bureau. Information can be fed from the micro by means of printed data that has to be entered into the other computer, but a more efficient way is to effect this transfer electronically.

Modelling

Personnel managers are finding computerized mathematical models increasingly valuable in areas such as salary and wage administration and manpower planning. Useful salary and wage system models can easily be developed using the 'spreadsheet' packages available for micro-computers. The packages are extensively used in financial modelling but have great potential for applications in personnel management.

The 'spreadsheet' is based on a matrix of boxes (known as cells) arranged in rows and columns. Numbers can be entered in each cell and mathematical relationships between cells established. For example, the values in a number of cells can be added together and the total given in another cell. Text may also be entered so that cells can be labelled to make the model easier to use.

Figures 23 and 24 on pages 52 and 53 show an example of a simple wage model set up using a spreadsheet package. In figure 23 information about each plant has been entered and overtime pay, total weekly wage and total wage bill have been calculated by the model. Figure 24 shows the new totals after normal hours of work have been reduced to 38 hours per week in all plants, with no increase in the overtime working.

This simple example shows the power and ease of use of a spreadsheet model. The effects of altering one factor in a complicated system are automatically reflected in the calculations connected to it. 'What if?' questions can be quickly answered without the need for lengthy manual calculations. In the example shown it would be a simple matter to establish the effect on total wage bill of wage increases in particular plants, changes in the overtime premium, increases and decreases in the number of staff and so on.

MANPOWER PLANNING

In the field of manpower planning specialized computer models have been developed. The Institute of Manpower Studies (IMS) provides a library of models as part of their advisory service on manpower management. The IMS claim that manpower models will enable an organization to:

1 look at or simulate the behaviour of its manpower system by identifying and representing manpower flows ie recruitment, promotion, wastage etc, both within the organization and between it and the external labour market.

2 plan balanced career structures

3 examine the impact of changes to such key variables as wastage and growth.

A variety of manpower models is available so that companies can use those which represent the particular way their organization works and which have an appropriate level of detail. The models may be purchased outright as a 'package' or accessed on a computer bureau.

Both types of model are readily available to personnel managers as they are 'user-friendly' and require no specialized computer knowledge for their operation.

Employee development and training

Micro-computers are also being used in employee development and training and there are two distinct applications in this area.

First, employee development records can be maintained by micro-computer systems holding data such as qualifications, job history and experience, training courses and details of succession plans. Such systems can either be an extension to general personnel records or can be a separate system. In either case the employee development records are used as a source of information about employees' expertise, skills, performance and potential which can be used to identify suitable candidates for jobs and assist in developing career paths.

Information about an employee's potential, and the organization's intentions towards that individual, are regarded as being particularly sensitive data. This has resulted in organizations with main-frame computer systems preferring to use a micro-computer for their employee development records because, they argue, the physical security of the data is more easily assured.

Figure 23
Basic wage calculation model

	PLANT	BASIC RATE (A)	NORMAL HOURS (B)	BASIC WEEKLY WAGE (C) $=(A \times B)$	ALLOW-ANCES (D)	AVERAGE O/TIME HOURS (E)	O/TIME PREMIA (F)	O/TIME PAY (G) $=(A \times F \times E)$	TOTAL WEEKLY WAGE (H) $=(C+G)$	NO. OF EMPLOYEES (I)	TOTAL WAGE BILL (J) $=(I \times H)$
1											
2											
3											
4											
5											
6											
7											
8	MANCHESTER	2.50	40.00	100.00	6.00	0.00	1.50	00.00	100.00	30.00	3000.00
9	BIRMINGHAM	2.40	39.00	93.60	5.00	5.00	1.50	18.00	111.60	50.00	5580.00
10	LONDON	2.50	39.00	97.50	12.00	7.00	1.50	26.25	123.75	45.00	5568.75
11	BRISTOL	2.30	40.00	92.00	6.00	3.00	1.50	10.35	102.35	12.00	1228.20
12	BRIGHTON	2.45	40.00	98.00	6.00	3.00	1.50	11.03	109.03	20.00	2180.50
13											
14										GRAND TOTAL	17557.45
15											
16											

Figure 24
Example of amended wage calculations

PLANT	BASIC RATE (A)	NORMAL HOURS (B)	BASIC WEEKLY WAGE (C) =(A×B)	ALLOW-ANCES (D)	AVERAGE O/TIME HOURS (E)	O/TIME PREMIA (F)	O/TIME PAY (G) =(A×F×E)	TOTAL WEEKLY WAGE (H) =(C+G)	NO. OF EMPLOYEES (I)	TOTAL WAGE BILL (J) =(I×H)
MANCHESTER	2.50	38.00	95.00	6.00	0.00	1.50	00.00	95.00	30.00	2850.00
BIRMINGHAM	2.40	38.00	91.20	5.00	5.00	1.50	18.00	109.20	50.00	5460.00
LONDON	2.50	38.00	95.00	12.00	7.00	1.50	26.25	121.25	45.00	5456.25
BRISTOL	2.30	38.00	87.40	6.00	3.00	1.50	10.35	97.75	12.00	1173.00
BRIGHTON	2.45	38.00	93.10	6.00	3.00	1.50	11.03	104.13	20.00	2082.50
								GRAND TOTAL		17021.75

The second application is computer-based training, also known as 'CBT'. This is a wide and fast developing field and can only be considered briefly here. However, personnel professionals should be aware of the potential of micro-computers in computer based training. Until recently, CBT has been an area dominated by main-frame computer systems; however the development of micro-computers has led to the production of micro-based CBT systems.

Typically, a CBT program is divided into progressive sections. By enabling the trainee to log-in and log-out at will, always returning to the point previously reached, the trainee can organize his own training. The CBT system interacts with the trainee by asking questions and providing alternative answers. The reasoning behind a correct answer can be given and remedial sections built in after wrong answers are given.

Micro-computer based CBT is proving valuable in dealing with the training of staff in remote locations. The course material can be distributed with ease using 'floppy discs'. In addition, the development of video equipment has led to it being linked to computer equipment to provide 'interactive video' training. The video facility can produce realistic images and simulations quickly and cheaply.

Recruitment

A micro-computer system can assist in the recruitment process by combining record keeping and the production of standard letters. The use of 'stand-alone' word processors in recruitment administration is well established but systems are now available which automatically produce the required letters to candidates as the recruitment records are updated.

One such system was developed initially for use in the graduate 'milk-round' but has been adapted for more general use. The system keeps a record of each candidate, holding information such as:

surnames, forenames, initials and title

permanent address

temporary address

sex

qualifications

name of interviewers, date, time and location of interviews

position applied for.

An individual's record can be quickly accessed, in response to a telephone enquiry, by the candidate for example. A check to establish whether a candidate has previously applied to the company can be run.

As correspondence has to be sent to each candidate the individual records are updated and the letters are automatically produced. The system takes the required data from each record as required.

One advantage of a computerized system is the ease with which extensive management reports and analyses of the recruitment exercises can be produced, for example a report showing the number of days which have elapsed since the last contact with the candidate. In order to analyse the recruitment process over a period of time it is possible to archive information once a recruitment exercise has been concluded.

Word processing

Word processors have been recognized as powerful machines by many personnel administrators. The word processor has traditionally been seen as a different type of machine from main-frame, mini- and micro-computers but this differentiation is now becoming less clear. 'Stand-alone' or 'dedicated' word processors, which are used only for word processing, have been available for many years.

Users of micro-computers now have the opportunity to use their machines for word processing due to the development of special software packages. Such packages are usually very powerful, offering many of the facilities available on 'dedicated' word processors. However, micro-computer based systems have not been as easy to operate as the 'dedicated' systems and micro-computers have not been a popular alternative to the 'dedicated' machine where word processing is a major requirement. However, the advantage of using a micro-computer for word processing is that it can be used for a number of other functions as well. In a personnel department the facility to integrate a word processing system with a personnel records system is very valuable. The development of word processing equipment now gives a further alternative by making it possible to purchase a word processor which also has the capability to run other software packages. The advantage of this approach is the linking of the power and ease of use of a 'dedicated' word processor with the micro-computers' ability to run a number of different systems. To gain maximum flexibility from this approach the word processor should be capable of accepting software packages running under the common micro-computer operating systems such as C/PM and MS-DOS.

Word processing systems available on both 'dedicated' machines and micro-computers contain the following types of facilities:

1 text entry and editing

2 form letters and list-merge facilities

3 assembly of documents using standard paragraphs.

TEXT ENTRY AND EDITING

Text entry and editing is the basic use of any word processing system. The operator entering information to the system uses a keyboard and the document is displayed on a visual display screen. This facility will be used to produce many types of document from single page letters to reports and manuals many pages long.

The system will require the operator to name a new document for future reference and may also allow some description of the document to be entered. This information will be held in an index of the documents held on a particular 'floppy' or 'hard' disc. The format of the document, margins, tabs, line spacing and character spacing may also be set. Frequently the word processing system will have a 'word-wrap' facility. This enables an operator to enter text without having to use a 'carriage-return' at the end of each line of text.

56

Once text has been entered and a document established it can be amended in one of three ways:

1 new text can be entered to over-write parts of the existing text

2 parts of the existing text can be deleted

3 new text can be inserted between parts of the existing text.

The system will also have a number of other functions to assist in creating a document. Amongst the most common facilities are centring a line of text on a page, underlining and bold print, copying and moving text within a document, justifying right and left margins and amending the format of a document.

Some systems have a 'numeric tab' to assist with the typing of a column of numbers. Typically, this will enable numbers to be automatically aligned on a decimal point. A mathematics function may be provided for use with statistical material. This can be used to check calculations for accuracy as they are entered. A good mathematics function on a word processor will allow numbers arranged in columns or rows to be added, subtracted, multiplied or divided. The facility to calculate percentages and to carry out calculations using numbers embedded in the text may also be available.

When producing reports the facility to number pages automatically is useful, particularly when revisions and additions will be required. It may also be possible to protect a table or chart to ensure that the material is not split between pages when the document is printed.

Many systems enable the user to search for a particular word or string of characters within a document. This facility may be extended to allow the automatic replacement of a set phrase by another. For instance, within a document the word processor could replace the phrase 'Amalgamated Union of Operatives' with 'National Union of Workers' whenever the former phrase appeared in the document.

For the production of policy manuals and similar documents some systems are able to automatically produce tables of contents, generate an index and number paragraphs.

On occasion a name or date must be typed at the top or bottom of every page. Some word processing systems will print such 'headers' and 'footers' on each page and indeed may be able to print different information on odd and even numbered pages.

One of the most powerful features of a word processor is its capabilities for producing repetitive letters. A 'form letter' is created by including markers, showing where variable information is to be inserted in the body of the letter. An example is a letter calling candidates for interview. When required, the form letter is called up on the visual display screen and the operator can tab from marker to marker inserting information as required.

A 'list-merge' facility speeds the production of repetitive letters still further. The first step is to create a 'form letter' as described above. The next step is to create a list of information consisting of a number of records, one record for each letter. Within each record there will be fields of information such as surname, initials, title, address, job applied for, interview time and date.

The word processor takes the list of information and merges it with the form letter, producing an individual letter for each record in the list. The fields of information are frequently used in the same order as they occur in the record. A more sophisticated list-merge enables the selection of particular fields within a record so that information can be used more than once in a letter or can be ignored.

If a word processing system with a list-merge facility is integrated with a personnel records system then the production of standard letters can be automated. A simple example occurs in a personnel department that needs to write to each of its employees with more than five years' service and wishes to send the letters to the employees' home address. After setting up a form letter the personnel records system could be used to identify those employees with the requisite service and to create a list of information from the data held in their personnel record. Each record might contain title, initials, surname, and address. The list of information can then be merged with the form letter by the word processor and individual letters produced.

ASSEMBLY OF DOCUMENTS USING STANDARD PARAGRAPHS

The ability to assemble documents is also known as 'cut and paste'. It involves creating blocks of text which can then be inserted into a document. A simple use of this technique involves the creation of blocks consisting of the closing and signature line of a letter. This block is given as identification and then can be used as often as required without retyping.

Documents, such as offer letters, can be easily produced using this facility. The operator calls up the blocks of text as required for each letter. For example, in an 'offer letter' to a sales representative the standard paragraphs relating to a job specification, company car and sales incentive scheme would be used. In an offer letter to a junior member of staff standard text about luncheon vouchers and flexible working hours could be included; and to a senior manager details of 'status' company cars, medical insurance and the executive bonus scheme could be included.

4 :: Using the system

Determine the information to be held

The key to the success of installing a micro-computer based personnel administration system is determining what information should be kept. Developing a general personnel records system causes the greatest difficulty because so much data is potentially available about each individual employed by an organization.

Certain items of information would be regarded as essential by almost all personnel administrators: name, home address, the date continuous service began and salary or wage rate, for example. Other items would be required by relatively few record systems. Shoe size, for example, would not be considered necessary by most organizations but would be a useful piece of information for a personnel department responsible for the ordering and distribution of safety shoes.

When developing a personnel records system the personnel administrator should seek to achieve a balance between maintaining the capability to deal with unusual 'one-off' enquiries and the maintenance of unnecessary records. There is a temptation to include all the items of information which can be envisaged in a new records system. Consideration should be given to the following points when deciding whether to include a particular item of information:

1 why is this information required?

2 how will this information be collected and loaded on to the record keeping system?

3 how will the information be kept up to date?

4 how frequently will the information be required?

A typical application of a computerized personnel records system is the identification of a group of employees who meet some criteria. For example, the selection of all the engineers who are unmarried and able to speak Arabic. If the record system holds information about profession or job family, marital status and foreign languages spoken, the personnel department should quickly be able to identify those employees who can meet the requirements. The costs of being able to tackle the problem are:

1 collecting and loading the information
2 operating administrative systems to ensure that the records are kept up to date since the maintenance of accurate records is essential.

The personnel manager must balance the cost of establishing and maintaining the information with the benefit of being able to provide immediate answers. Obviously this balance will be heavily influenced by how frequently the problem occurs.

A typical computerized record system could include the information itemized in figure 25 on page 62. It is not an exhaustive list but may serve as a starting point when developing a system.

Historical records such as job and salary histories are frequently required. Sophisticated micro-computer based systems are able to automatically create a 'history record' when fields such as annual salary are amended. Loading historical information to a new computerized system can be a time-consuming task. The need for historical data must be assessed and the period of time for which information is held by the system evaluated. There is a penalty in keeping vast historical records on computerized systems, and this is particularly noticeable in micro-computer systems. The historical data takes up a great deal of space on the floppy or hard discs used for storage and can slow down the system by delaying the retrieval of information. As with other data recorded by the personnel system, some consideration must be given to the costs as opposed to the benefits of retaining the information.

In the case study described in chapter 5 the company concerned employed a consultant to assist in the development of their records system. The list of information was developed very carefully and in close collaboration with the personnel manage-

Figure 25
Suggested list of items to be stored on a personnel records system

Payroll number, employee number

Surname, forename(s), title and initials

Sex and marital status

National insurance number

Home address and telephone number

Details of next of kin

Details of immediate family

Date of birth

Date continuous service commenced

Date present position taken up

Nationality

Job title, job coding

Location, department, cost centre

Salary/job grade

Salary scale and increments

Salary, wage, hourly pay rate

Location allowance

Profit sharing, incentive and other bonuses

Full/part-time, number of hours worked

Shift pattern

Pension scheme membership

Company car details

Medical insurance scheme membership

Company credit cards

Company loans and mortgages

Date of last/next medical examination

Special contract terms, service agreements, notice periods

Disciplinary record

Sickness and other absence details

Statutory sick pay and occupational sick pay

Holiday entitlements

Special leave

Registered disabled person

Trade union membership

First aid certificate

Educational qualifications

School, college, university

Professional qualifications, apprenticeships served

Languages spoken

Training courses undertaken

Performance appraisal, promotion and potential data

Method of recruitment

Career history

Salary history

ment department. Despite this at least one redundant item was included, 'recruitment method'. Once the system was established the reason for including this field was not clear to those operating it. Clearly, this data would be of value to many organizations but, in the company concerned, there was neither a requirement to analyse the data nor a mechanism to collect it.

Many micro-computer based records systems have the facility to delete fields of information from the system and to add new fields after the system is established. Therefore all is not necessarily lost if a mistake is made when the system is installed. Indeed a personnel department with such a system could adopt a strategy of developing a basic records system and adding additional information at a later date. (See, for example, chapter 6).

Data protection

Personnel managers have always been concerned to safeguard the personal information held about individuals in their records and this is one of the basic disciplines of any personnel department. This responsibility to protect personal data has been unaffected by the method of storing information, whether in filing cabinets or on a computer.

However, the rapid development of computers with the ability to process and link information about individuals at high speed has caused concern that these machines could be misused in such a way as to threaten the privacy of individuals. This has led to a Convention on Data Protection prepared by the Council of Europe and, latterly, to the UK Government's 1982 white paper *Data Protection The Government's Proposals for Legislation* and the resulting bill.

When the data protection legislation comes into effect it will apply to computerized personnel records systems and therefore must be taken into account by personnel managers using existing systems and developing new ones. It is important to stress that the proposals apply to *computerized* systems and not to manual records.

The Government has proposed eight principles for data protection:

1 Personal data shall be obtained and processed fairly and lawfully

2 Personal data shall be held for specified and lawful purposes only

3 Personal data shall not be used or disclosed in any manner incompatible with those purposes

4 Personal data shall be adequate, relevant and not excessive in relation to the specified purposes

5 Personal data shall be accurate and, where necessary, kept up to date

6 Personal data shall not be kept for longer than is necessary

7 An individual shall be entitled:
   a at reasonable intervals, and without undue delay or expense, to be informed by any data user if they hold personal data concerning him or her and to have access to any such data,
   b where appropriate, to have such data corrected or erased.

8 Appropriate security measures shall be taken to prevent unauthorized access to, alteration, disclosure or destruction of, personal data and to prevent accidental loss.

The seventh principle, dealing with the right of access to personal data, is the most significant for personnel managers. Employees will be entitled to have access to data held about them in a computerized records system; however this right is restricted by the definition of 'personal data' for statutory purposes which is as follows:

Personal data is information which relates to a living individual who can be identified from the information, including any expression of opinion about the individual but not any indication of the intentions of the data user in respect of that individual.

The Institute of Personnel Management has been concerned with the implications of the right of access to personal data in such areas as appraisal schemes and career and succession plans. It is in these areas that most uncertainty about the effects of the data protection legislation exists. It is clear that appraisal ratings will be subject to access by the employee because these are expressions of opinion about past performance. It is also apparent that a planned salary review will not be subject to access because it is quite clearly an intention of the data user. However, much career and succession planning information is within a 'grey area' where opinions about plans and intentions are expressed.

To illustrate this point, consider the items a manager might use in a review of the potential of staff within his area: an assessment of the most senior level an individual might reach in the next 10 years; the positions which the individual might be appointed to as his/her next job move and the timescale for such a move; any training or job experience which might be required to assist the individual achieve his/her potential. All these items involve the manager expressing an opinion about the employee, but it can also be argued that they constitute an 'indication of the intentions' of the organization towards the individual. At present it is not clear whether such information, if held on a computerized system, will be subject to the provisions of the data protection legislation. The principles of data protection will be enforced by a registrar who will maintain a register of personal data users and computer bureaux and will also have powers to ensure that personal data is used only in accordance with the eight principles. A data user who wishes to dispute a decision of the registrar will have access to an appeal tribunal. Grey areas of interpretation will be clarified once some case law has been established.

Design of data screens

On a micro-computer system, data is entered to the database via a VDU screen. In a well-designed system this labour intensive exercise will be made as simple as possible so that the user genuinely finds the system an improvement on his previous system. Each item of data, eg surname, salary etc, is held in a data 'field' and a number of these fields will be displayed on the screen

65

at any one time. Each such group of fields will be said to form a 'data screen'. There is quite an art in arranging the data fields into screens so that the entry, search and amendment of data is as efficient as possible. For example, compromises have to be made between clustering together all the data fields that are normally of personnel interest and clustering all those that would normally constitute the base information when details of a new employee have to be entered.

The next question to be addressed concerns the space allowed for each item of data. Fields such as 'surname' and 'address' where the data is unique must be large enough to cope with any size of such information. On the other hand, a field such as 'sports club contribution', which will be one of a set of payroll deductions and will be relevant for a number of employees, could be replaced by some sort of code. Codes are used both in the database storage, to save space on the disc, and on the data screens, to make the screens neater and to allow more fields displayed. Naturally, the user will not want to have his reports to be full of codes since the recipients of the information may not have a 'code book' and, in any case, will want to be able to read understandable documents in plain English. The computer system will accomplish this by retaining a table, or index, file which relates numbers to words, eg job title '836' will be transformed to 'branch cost accountant'.

DATA ENTRY

There are two main methods of entering data via the VDU screen: 'question and answer' and 'pro-forma'. With the 'question and answer' method the user enters one data field at a time and is invited to review his entries either after each response or after a group of questions have been answered. Figure 26 demonstrates this method with the user's responses in bold lettering. Note that certain key fields, such as name, are double checked before the input process continues.

Figure 27 illustrates the pro-forma approach where all data field descriptions are permanently displayed and the user chooses the fields he requires by moving the entry cursor around the screen. The same example is used. Note that the name is displayed by the computer after the user has typed in the personnel number.

66

Figure 26

Example of 'question and answer' data input

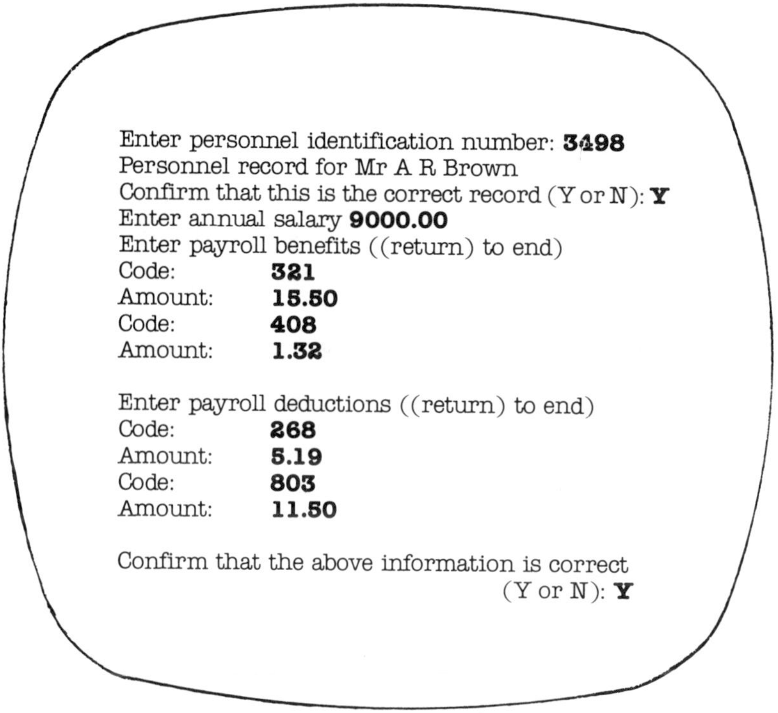

```
Enter personnel identification number: 3498
Personnel record for Mr A R Brown
Confirm that this is the correct record (Y or N): Y
Enter annual salary 9000.00
Enter payroll benefits ((return) to end)
Code:        321
Amount:      15.50
Code:        408
Amount:      1.32

Enter payroll deductions ((return) to end)
Code:        268
Amount:      5.19
Code:        803
Amount:      11.50

Confirm that the above information is correct
                          (Y or N): Y
```

Both methods of data entry have their advantages and disadvantages. With the question and answer approach the user can concentrate on one data field at a time without the distraction of other words around the screen. On the other hand, this method is quite slow because there is a delay while each new question is written to the screen. A further disadvantage is that the sequence of questions is pre-set and, at any one time, many of these may not be relevant, thereby causing further delays.

The pro-forma method is much neater and more efficient since the user can see all the relevant data fields displayed and choose just those in which he is interested. For reasons of clarity, figure 27 shows only the fields used in the example whereas in practice the screen would display a greater range of information similar to the example in figure 29 on page 71.

Figure 27
Example of pro-forma data input

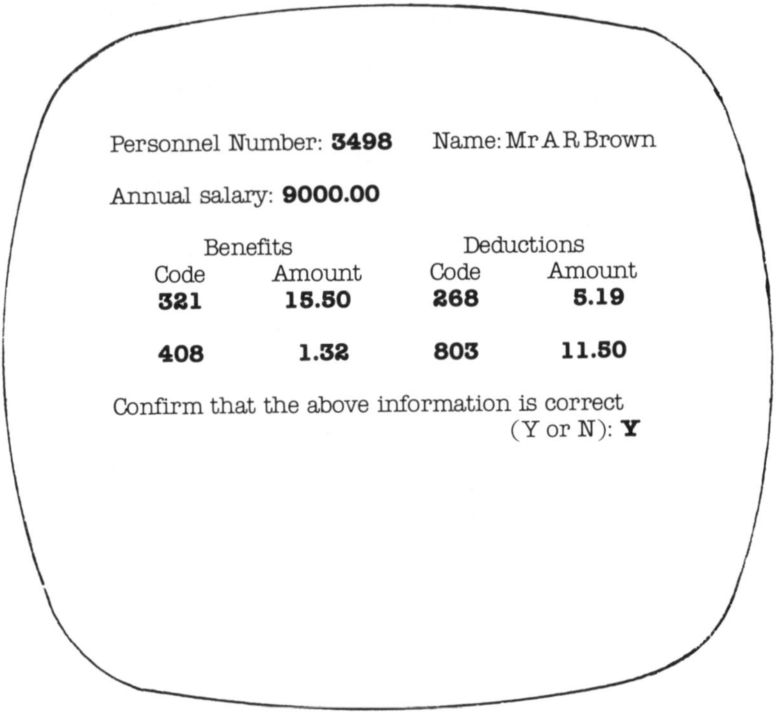

DATA CHECKING

In addition to the request to confirm the accuracy of the data entered, the system itself can be programmed to carry out consistency checks. These fall into two broad categories, range checks and compatibility checks.

Examples of range checks:

Sex: M or F

Marital Status: S, M, D or W

Annual Salary: 1000.00–100,000.00

Job Code: 301–699

Examples of compatibility checks:

Job grade 'J' implies salary in the range 7,000–8,999

Payment method 'B' (for BACS) requires a valid bank account number to be entered.

It is very important that the system allows the user to over-ride these checks where appropriate. For example, there may be special reasons for allowing an annual salary of less than £1000 for a regular part-time employee but it would probably not be appropriate to categorize an employee's sex as other than M or F!

HISTORY RECORDS

In a manual personnel system, an employee's record card will contain details of his progress with the organization. Changes in salary, function, location, status, etc, will be recorded so that a career profile can be built up.

In a computerized system, such a history can also be generated. The user will nominate certain important data fields and each change to the information in these fields will automatically create a new entry on a history profile. Figure 28 on page 70 illustrates a typical history data screen.

DATA EXAMINATION AND AMENDMENTS

The amount of personnel data held for any individual will usually be too great for it all to be displayed simultaneously on a VDU screen. Consequently, data fields are grouped into relevant sets and the user can either look at each 'data screen' in turn or home in on one such data screen for a particular purpose. The problems of clustering the data fields efficiently have already been mentioned and one solution to this is given in figures 29, 30 and 31 where the initial data input screen for a new employee is split into two data screens for subsequent specialized data amendments.

Moving around the data base from one data-screen to another can be facilitated by the use of the function keys that are present

Figure 28
Example of screen of history data

Figure 28
Example of screen of history data

Personnel Number: 3498   Name: Mr A R Brown

History Profile

Date	Salary	Dept	Job Code	Status	Location	Car	Reason Code
1/11/83	9000.00						30
1/4/83			398	5	14	3	28
1/11/82	8500.00						30

on most modern keyboards. A menu of their operations can be displayed at the bottom of the VDU screen and in a well-designed system their usage would be consistent. The following list shows an example of the types of operation for which the function keys could be used.

F1 =next screen	F2 =previous screen	F3 =first screen
F4 =input completed	F6 =abandon record	F7 =delete field
F8 =print screen	F9 =abandon option	

GLOBAL AMENDMENTS

There will be times when the user wishes to alter the contents of the same data field on many (or all) employees' records. In these

70

Figure 29
Example of combined data screen

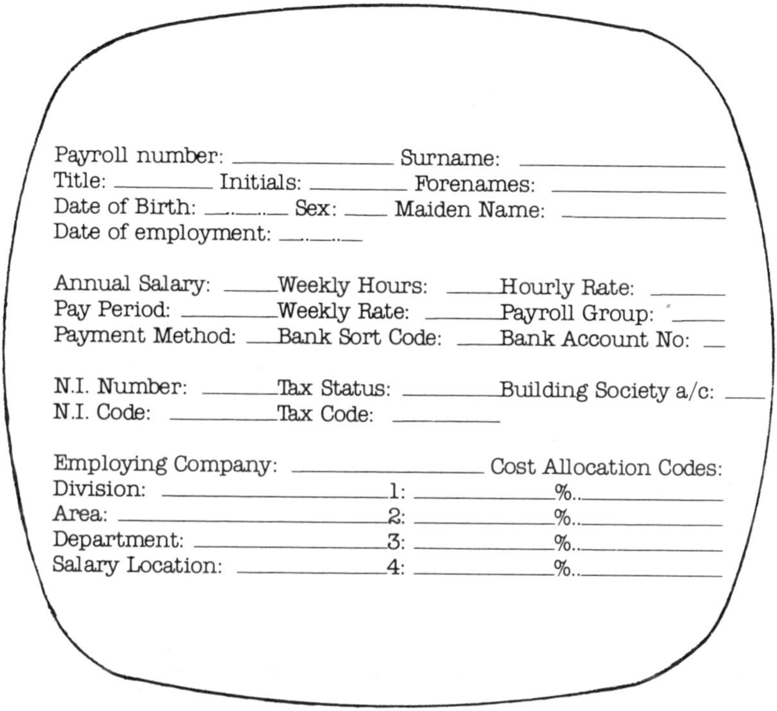

cases it would be tedious to call up each record in turn and, each time, step through the data screens and then position the cursor to the right spot on the screen. The system should provide more efficient facilities for this type of operation and two approaches are 'global amendments' and 'table amendments'. In the former, the user nominates a data field, eg 'tax code', and the surname or identification number of the first employee whose tax code is to be amended. The system will automatically display the correct data screen and position the cursor at the relevant data field. After amending the data the user will then be given a choice of either moving on to the next stored record (which will often be in identification number order) where the process is repeated, or nominating another specific employee.

The table amendments procedure is used in cases where a similar change to the value of a specific data field on all employee

Figure 30
Partial split of data screen – part 1

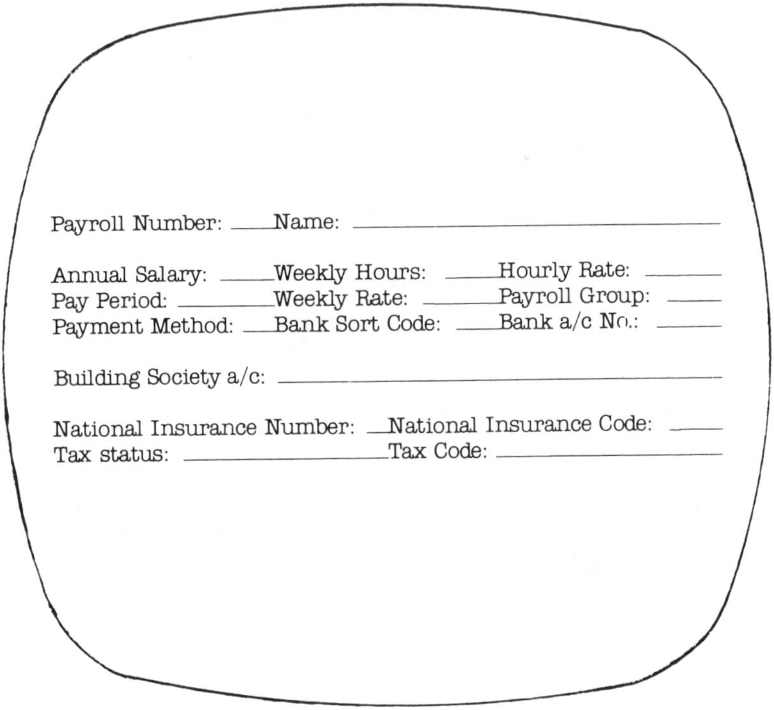

Payroll Number: ___Name: _____

Annual Salary: ___Weekly Hours: ___Hourly Rate: _____
Pay Period: _____Weekly Rate: _____Payroll Group: ___
Payment Method: __Bank Sort Code: __Bank a/c No.: _____

Building Society a/c: _____

National Insurance Number: __National Insurance Code: ____
Tax status: _____Tax Code: _____

records has to be made. An example of this is the updating of *all* tax codes following a governmental budget announcement. In this instance all tax codes with prefix H, for example, will be increased or decreased by a set amount, and similarly for other prefices.

Data security

Personnel data includes sensitive and confidential information and it is important that a computerized system contains sufficient security checks. First, each person having access to the system must have a password and it is recommended that only one senior manager has the ability to issue and amend passwords. Secondly, each user must be allocated certain rights concerning the system.

Figure 31
Partial split of data screen – part 2

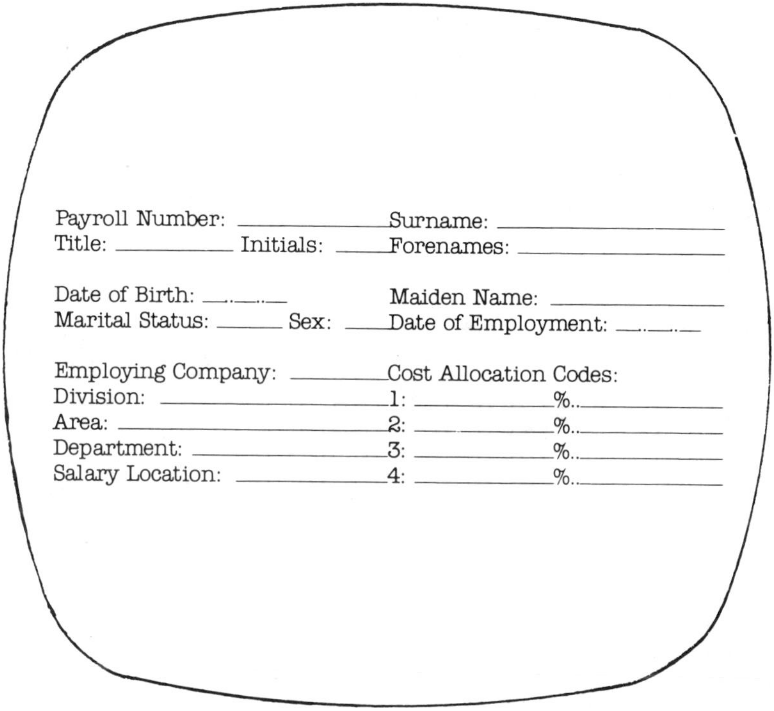

Examples of these rights, of which an individual may be alloted any combination are:

examine data and print reports

add/delete employee

amend personnel details

amend payroll details

carry out system supervisory tasks

administer statutory sick pay

run payroll.

Typically, examination of records will be open to all authorized users of the system. In addition, a payroll clerk will be allowed to amend payroll details and run the payroll, whereas a personnel administrator will be allowed to add/delete an employee, amend personnel details and administer statutory sick pay.

The separation of amendments to payroll and personnel records (as in figures 30 and 31 on pages 72 and 73) is not just for administrative reasons but is also a common audit requirement. Auditors usually insist that access to financial information is closely defined and that responsibility for amendments to such data can be properly traced. This latter requirement is catered for by the provision of a facility for a senior officer to be able to carry out certain supervisory tasks. Among these are:

entering cumulatives to payroll record when a new employee joins

modifying history records

updating tax codes

running end of period procedures

administering the log of system usage.

It is quite important to keep a record of the usage made of the system and this is usually achieved by means of a system log. This will typically record details of:

name of user

date and time of use

facilities used

changes made to information on the database.

In this way, the supervisor can check that the system is not being abused. A permanent record of usage is provided by regular prints of the system log which can be stored for examination by auditors and others.

Design of printed reports

Reports fall into five categories:

payroll analysis reports

occasional financial reports

regular personnel reports

other personnel reports

statutory reports.

Examples of these are given below but first it is important to set down some basic rules concerning the choice and design of reports. The first step is to establish what information is needed and by whom. In many existing systems, whether manual or computerized, voluminous reports are produced and distributed and no check is carried out of the use, if any, that is made of the information contained in them. It is often educational to stop the distribution of all reports for a suitable length of time to determine who is genuinely missing the information. Having established who needs information from the system, it is advisable to discuss with them exactly what information they require and how they would like it presented.

The next stage is to assemble all the pieces of information demanded and to group them together to produce coherent reports. For example, payroll analysis reports range from a summary report suitable for updating the nominal ledger (see figure 32 on page 76) through a cost centre report for more detailed accounting purposes (see figure 33 on page 77) to a series of reports describing the payroll deductions (see figure 34 on page 77).

An example of an occasional financial report is the listing, in alphabetical order, of all employees and their tax codes. This is given annually to the PAYE authorities.

Regular employee reports might include a headcount or work strength report either by department or broken down into smaller work units and a report listing all starters and leavers in a given period.

Other personnel reports can be split into those for which the format is fixed and those which, by their individual nature, cannot be pre-determined. An example of the former is a report that would be printed before a salary review is carried out. This will list each employee's relevant financial details together with his job title and grade and, possibly, his most recent history of salary increases.

Ad hoc reports are usually the result of a request to provide specific information about specific groupings of employees. These will be described in the next section, on page 78. A useful report is one which shows details of an individual employee's record. This

Figure 32
Nominal ledger information

```
                              3/9/1983

                           Payroll Analysis

                              Month 5

                            1  COMPANY A

      Employee Pay                   Company                        Deductions

Basic Pay           20733.66    NI            1829.98    Company Pension     51.06
Taxable Benefits       50.50    Pension        110.41    A.V.C               23.48
Non-Taxable Benefits    7.00                             Tax               5599.05
Statutory Sick Pay      0.00                             NI                1431.96
Sick Pay                0.00                             Other Deductions     19.80
Total               20791.16    Total         1940.39    Total             7125.35


              Total Company - (Employee Pay + Company)    22731.55

              Total Net      - (Employee Pay - Deductions)  13665.81


      Benefit Analysis                         Deduction Analysis

   103 Bonus            10.00            301 Miscellaneous        2.80
   104 Commission       15.00            302 BUPA                16.00
   111 Tool allowance   20.50            303 Sports + Social Club 1.00
   128 Shift Allowance   5.00
   201 Non-taxable pay   7.00


                              Cumulative Values

                 Brought Forward    Added    Carried Forward   Prev. Employment   All Employment

Gross Pay           85628.68      20791.16     106419.84
Company Pension       432.26         51.06        483.32
A.V.C.                197.33         23.48        220.81
NI Employee          5983.92       1431.96       7415.88
NI Employer          7794.45       1829.98       9624.43
Taxable Pay         84956.04      20709.32     105665.36          0.00            105665.36
Tax                 22798.00       5599.05      28397.05          0.00             28397.05
```

can be achieved either by printing a copy of one or more data screens or by requesting a summary of the information held. A copy of all the data screens provides the necessary 'hard copy' record card and this should be printed at least annually.

Statutory reports include all the usual end of year tax reports (relevant only where the personnel system is also used for payroll) and the statutory sick pay records. A novel method of reporting absence is by means of a calendar which shows all types of

Figure 33
Detailed accounting information

3/9/1983

Project Accounting Report

Month 5

1 COMPANY A

Cost Centre 100000

Payroll Number	Name			%	Basic Pay	Overtime	Bonus	Statutory Sick Pay	Other Pay	Total Pay	Company N.I.	Company Pension	Total Costs
62	MISS	VJ	COATES	50	241.66	0.00	0.00	0.00	0.00	241.66	27.67	0.00	269.33
21	MR	R	SHORT	100	1000.00	0.00	0.00	0.00	0.00	1000.00	114.50	17.33	1131.83
1	Mr	J	SMITH	50	291.67	0.00	5.00	0.00	12.50	309.17	25.61	12.41	347.19
54	MR	HB	SMITH	100	583.33	0.00	0.00	0.00	0.00	583.33	48.65	0.00	631.98
70	MR	D	WOOTTON	30	725.00	0.00	0.00	0.00	0.00	725.00	34.98	0.00	759.98
Totals for cost centre 100000					2841.66	0.00	5.00	0.00	12.50	2859.16	251.41	29.74	3140.31

Figure 34
Payroll deduction report

3/9/1983

Deductions Report

Month 5

302 Private Medical Scheme

1 COMPANY A

Number	Name			Amount
1	Mr	J	SMITH	, 4.00
5	MR	B	KENT	4.00
9	MR	J	DONNE	5.00
10	MR	JP	JONES	3.00
Total for company				16.00
Total for deduction 302				16.00

absence, but particularly that pertaining to statutory sick pay, that has been recorded during the previous month. Figure 35 on page 78 illustrates this method.

Figure 35
Statutory sick pay calendar report

```
                        Statutory Sick Pay Report

                            40 / 03 / 1984

                             1  COMPANY A


Payroll Number:     1                      Name:  Mr   J    SMITH


Qualifying days are: Monday Tuesday Wednesday Thursday Friday


                      Absence record for February


       Sunday    Monday   Tuesday  Wednesday Thursday Friday   Saturday
                                     1        2        3        4 N
        5 N       6 W      7 W       8 W       9 P     10 P     11 N
       12 N      13       14        15       16       17       18
       19        20       21        22       23       24       25
       26        27       28        29


Reason for transfer or exclusion:


Remarks:


SSP due for February :  16.10              Total SSP in weeks:  5.00
```

Enquiries and ad hoc reports

The aim of a personnel system is to extract information quickly. In a manual record system it is often necessary to look at each record card, jot down the information on a piece of paper and, after all the record cards have been read, collate the information and prepare a report. A computerized system should make the personnel officer's task infinitely easier.

When making an enquiry, the expression describing a criterion, as to whether or not any particular employee is to be selected, is made up of three parts: the data field which contains the information; a value (either numeric or descriptive); and a logical operator. These logical operators are:

Equal to (EQ)

Not equal to (NE)
Less than (LT)
Greater than (GT)
Less than or equal to (LE)
Greater than or equal to (GE)

An additional operator is 'IN' signifying that a descriptive value may occur anywhere in the stored data field.

A composite example, showing how the facility could operate, might be:

'Find all male employees between the ages of 21 and 40 as at 1/1/84 who are earning less than £8500.00 and who are employed as an accountant.'

This would be entered on a data enquiry screen as in figure 36 below.

Figure 36
Example of a data enquiry screen

Data Field	Logic	Value
Sex	EQ	M
Date of birth	LT	1/1/63
Date of birth	GE	1/1/44
Annual salary	LT	8500.00
Job title	IN	ACCOUNTANT

The system will identify all employees satisfying the criteria and the user will have the option to either examine their records or print a report containing key information about them.

If the system has a report generation facility, the user will be invited to design the report by designating column headings etc and by declaring if the records are to be sorted into any order based on an alphabetic field (eg surname) or a numeric field (eg salary). By this means, the user has the flexibility to have ad hoc reports in addition to those programmed into the system.

Training the user

Great emphasis is put on making 'user-friendly' systems for use by staff who are not data processing specialists. This approach has encouraged users of micro-computers to believe that all they have to do is plug 'the box' in and all their problems will disappear. In fact, user training is essential if the best use is to be made of the facility.

A formal training course in using a micro-computer package, run by a specialist organization or software dealer, has a number of advantages. First, it provides the opportunity to concentrate on the system away from the distractions of the day to day office routine. Secondly, many users find it difficult to learn to operate the system from the users' manual, especially if they have had no experience using micro-computers. Even simple instructions which were self-evident to the author of the users' manual such as 'press the return key' can confuse the naive user if the keyboard is not marked clearly. Thirdly, the course gives the new user an opportunity to discuss with some experienced operators the problems which will be encountered in his particular operation.

Obviously such public training courses will not be appropriate if a system has been specially written for a customer or if a package has been customized to meet specific needs. One of the items to be considered before commissioning such work should be the training and support provided by the software house once the system has been completed and installed.

All systems must be supplied with a users' manual which gives detailed instructions for its use. The manual is additional to training and many users of micro-computer systems have taught

80

themselves to use the system by studying it. Such attempts have not always been successful, however! The manual will be essential in operating the system no matter how the users have learnt the basics of using it. At first, frequent reference will be made to confirm basic points and procedures. Later it will be used when dealing with procedures which are complex or infrequently invoked.

Good training and documentation is important in gaining acceptance of the system by the staff who are to operate it.

Housekeeping and maintenance

Any personnel system, whether manual or computerized is only as competent as the accuracy of the information held. Consequently, it is imperative that the data be kept up to date. In addition, regular copies of the data should be made in case the system breaks down and the database has to be restored.

The frequency of these copies, or 'back-ups' as they are known, depends on the facilities available on the system. If payroll is included, the data should be copied immediately before a payroll run (ie after all transient data, such as 'hours worked', 'overtime', 'special benefits', have been entered) and immediately after the run (ie when all tax cumulatives etc have been updated).

If payroll is not included in the system, the data need only be copied once a month, say, or after a particularly intensive set of data entries or amendments.

The security copies will normally be made on to floppy discs (see page 28–30) and then removed from the premises and stored in another office or in a bank. In the case of a micro-computer that has no hard disc, the organization of the floppy discs becomes particularly crucial. The procedure is to keep two back-up copies stored at all times and this is often called the 'grandfather-father-son' method. The 'grandfather' is the oldest copy, the 'father' the latest copy and the 'son' is the current copy of the data in use.

A second method of copying data from micro-computer is by means of a tape streamer, which is a very fast cassette tape recording device. The machine could cost between £1,000 and £2,000 but it has the advantage of accommodating the whole of the data base whereas a number of floppy discs might be required to store the same amount of data.

In the course of a year there will be a number of starters and leavers. Consequently, the database will steadily grow and in time will include data records of employees no longer working for the organization. Where payroll is involved these records must be kept until the tax year end so that the P35s and P60s can be printed. After that, they can remain on the system or, more probably, be removed so that the database does not become so large that the system response slows down to an unacceptable level. The user has more flexibility in deciding when to purge leavers' records from a personnel only system but again it would be bad practice to keep the records on the system longer than necessary. Naturally, it is prudent to print a complete data record for any employee before his record is deleted!

In addition to keeping regular back-up copies of the database the user will also need to have security copies of the programs that constitute the system software. Since the programs will remain unchanged, except for commissioned changes, there will be no need for regular copies to be made. The user should have a copy given to him when the system is installed and the supplier will similarly keep a copy. These copies will be of the working system and will not be in a form whereby they can be altered. The authors of the program will have a copy of it in 'source' form and where the user buys the system direct from the authors it is recommended that a second copy of the program source is lodged with a third party such as a bank. This will give the user the ability to engage a replacement supplier in the event of the original supplier ceasing to trade or in the case of a serious breach of contract.

Micro-computers are maintained by specialist engineering companies. It is recommended that the supplier of the hardware makes all the necessary arrangements for adequate maintenance cover to be provided. It is desirable for a single maintenance company to be engaged to cover all the hardware. However, there are occasions where it is more cost-effective to have some of the hardware covered by a 'parts' insurance rather than a maintenance contract. It is advisable to take the advice of the hardware supplier on this matter.

Software maintenance is a contentious subject. Some program packages are sold on the condition that the user enters into an agreement that grants him a licence to use the package. This licence agreement absolves the original supplier (often a company in the USA) from nearly all responsibility for program failure. However, this usually applies only to packages that sell in thousands and have been fully tested. Specialist personnel systems for micro-computers, however, are normally supplied by the original authors and the user will take out an agreement with them covering the correction of faults and the provision of new or improved facilities. The agreement could be for an annual maintenance fee to be paid in advance or for all work to be invoiced, at a daily rate, in arrears. The optimum system is probably one where an annual fee is paid to cover error correction and all other work is charged at cost.

5 :: Case study–integrated system

Introduction

This case study follows the development, implementation and the use of a micro-computer based payroll and personnel system for a division of 1500 employees in a group of companies in the United Kingdom. The operating companies are largely autonomous, reflecting the group's management style which is to devolve management control to that level. This is further reflected in the size of the division's head office, just 20 staff, although divisional turnover was around £300 million in 1982.

Personnel administration is also a responsibility of the operating companies and so there is little centralized demand for personnel information. The division's personnel managers report to their respective managing directors, although they have a functional responsibility to the divisional manpower services manager. The divisional office provides a service to the operating companies and the new computer system provides a staff payroll as well as a personnel records facility which can be accessed by local personnel management.

Origins of the project

The division's head office took responsibility for the staff payroll following a major reorganization of the group in 1979. This reorganization included disbanding the group's centralized personnel and payroll departments. At this stage the existing computerized payroll and personnel records programs were transferred to a main-frame installation in one of the operating companies, along with the staff records for the division. This
84

hardware was compatible with the group's computer for which the programs had been developed and so minimum conversion was required. However the programs, which were written in a mixture of the PLAN and COBOL programming languages, were up to 20 years old and formed part of an integrated payroll/personnel/pensions system which had never been completed. Responsibility for the pensions records remained with a department at the group head office.

Although there was a facility for personnel records on the system the only use that could readily be made of them was to obtain a complete print-out of all the personnel information held for all the employees. Also, because of its age the existing system had no facility for any on-line processing or other inter-active enquiries. All requests for information had to be channelled through the data processing department where they were assigned a low priority after financial and operating applications.

The personnel departments in the operating companies found the computerized records system of no value to themselves. The computerized records were not kept up to date because there was no incentive to do so. Extensive manual personnel record systems were maintained but it was still difficult to meet even the fundamental needs for personnel information. For example, an exercise to identify those employees with at least three years service, or who had company cars, could take two weeks or more while operating companies were circularized, manual records searched and replies received. It was seldom practicable to provide this type of information from the computer records because a special program had to be written by one of the data processing staff.

Alterations in the payroll programs were in any case going to be required because of the proposed statutory changes. At the time the project began, it was thought that changes in the way 'benefits in kind' are taxed would be introduced. Although this did not happen, the proposals relating to statutory sick pay became a legal requirement and had to be included in payroll systems.

In addition, a change in the type of computer being used by the operating company was envisaged in the short to medium term. This was likely to involve a change to 'distributed' data processing, using micro- or mini-computers which would have required a complete re-programming of the existing systems.

Decision-making process

The divisional office started to examine alternative systems seriously early in 1981. The computer facility being used was managed by the operating company's finance department. Their needs with regard to both machine time and use of programming staff took priority. In addition there was a danger that confidentiality might be breached because data processing staff had potential access not only to payroll and personnel records for their own company but also to records held for other companies in the division.

As a result of this, an investigation was carried out to see if it would be feasible for the divisional office to have an independent facility. The first priority was the payroll but it was evident that there was a great deal of overlap between the payroll records and those manual records being kept by the personnel departments. It was felt that a system which integrated payroll and personnel would be the most efficient and since the divisional manpower services manager, who had functional responsibility for personnel, is also responsible for the staff payroll no organizational problems were envisaged.

STEP 2: WHAT TYPE OF SYSTEM TO USE?

At the outset it was felt that the costs of buying computer equipment would be prohibitive and that there was insufficient expertise and facilities to operate it. Therefore the first step was to examine what was being offered by various computer bureaux. Some very sophisticated software was available; however the systems did not integrate payroll and personnel (although such systems are now available). Concern was expressed at the cost of operating the systems and it was felt that in many instances facilities would be charged which were unlikely to be used. The cost of running the payroll, which at the time consisted of only 1,000 staff, was around £3,500 per annum.

The likely running costs of personnel systems were difficult to establish. The experience of other users of personnel systems contacted indicated that bureau charges would increase beyond the level originally budgeted. Common experience suggested that the computer facility was generally used more than was originally envisaged and that in the medium to long term having an in-house installation would prove to be more cost effective.

However, the option of using a bureau possibly for payroll only seemed to be the only solution until a visit to one of the computer exhibitions revealed how powerful the low cost micro-computers had become. The recognition that 'silicon chip technology' could be applied to the tasks under investigation proved to be the key to the project.

STEP 3: IDENTIFYING A SUITABLE MICRO-COMPUTER SYSTEM

After agreeing that a micro-computer based system might be the answer it was then necessary to confront the two problems of finding suitable hardware and appropriate software.

At this stage of the project there was a baffling array of alternatives. There proved to be a wide variety of apparently suitable equipment available, ranging from small 'personal' micros up to small mini-computers costing tens of thousands of pounds. At the micro-computer end of the market there were various small scale payroll packages but no specialized personnel systems. The only programs available were generalized database management systems. Sophisticated software was available for the mini-computer systems but this option appeared to be very expensive.

Almost without exception the sales representatives concerned with micro-computer hardware claimed that their equipment would be suitable, but it seemed that where the software was available it was not capable of meeting the defined objectives. No in-house expertise was available, so a consultant was engaged. In retrospect, this course of action is strongly recommended to any personnel professional involved in establishing a computerized system.

STEP 4: BRIEFING THE CONSULTANT

The consultant's brief was to question the conclusions already drawn and he was asked to advise the division on:

1 whether it would be cost effective to improve on the existing system, taking into account the likely changes in both statutory requirements and the hardware available

2 the alternative services and equipment capable of satisfying current and future needs and the costs involved.

The parameters given to the consultant to work within were as follows:

Size of the system
A possible growth was envisaged in the numbers of staff from 1,000 to 3,500 to be catered for by the payroll, because of the division's policy of acquiring new businesses.

Security of the system
The programs had to prevent unauthorized access to the system. Personnel management had to be allowed to interrogate the records held on employees in their own company without gaining access to the records for the employees in other companies. In addition the system had to enable security back-up copies of the records to be created which could be stored away from the computer system.

Automated payment of salaries
The new system would need to pay salaries using the Banks Automated Clearing Services (BACS). This service was already used by the existing payroll and the low charges (about 2.5p per transaction) as well as the cash flow advantages to companies made it important that BACS was retained.

Personnel records system
The system should be able to integrate personnel records with the payroll records. A simple system for interrogation was required to enable the selection of particular records according to parameters such as age, job code, service etc.

Computer expertise required
The divisional office had no data processing staff and it was specified that operation of the system should require no knowledge of computer programming.

Word processing facility
Word processing was identified as a potential secondary use of the equipment and the feasibility of including this facility along with the payroll/personnel requirements was included in the brief.

STEP 5: THE CONSULTANT'S REPORT AND PURCHASE OF EQUIPMENT

The consultant's report recommended the use of a business micro-computer. However no suitable integrated payroll and personnel systems were then available and it was suggested that such a system could be profitably developed for our use and that other companies might have similar requirements.

Initially it was envisaged that the system would be developed by a software house which had expertise in either payroll or personnel and could add to an existing system. However a combination of the apparent unreliability of some software houses and tight deadlines led the division to decide to fund the development itself and to ask the consultant to form a team to undertake the work.

The consultant recommended that the choice of computer be limited to models which supported the popular CP/M (single user) or MP/M (multi-user) operating systems. These are used by the majority of makes of 8-bit micro-computers so that the programs would be readily transferable to other computers should the need arise.

When considering the capabilities of the computer the division looked to the consultant for advice. Obviously part of his feasibility study was to investigate what type and size of records were needed to be stored and processed. The division had to depend entirely on his expertise in this field. His conclusions were based on, among other considerations, interviews with the company personnel managers to determine their needs for information, with the salaries manager and various company accountants to determine what standard reports were required.

The actual choice of computer within those supporting CP/M and MP/M was limited by the media which were acceptable to BACS for the transmission of payroll data. The simplest method of transmitting such data to the banks from a micro was by floppy discs. However the only size of floppy disc accepted by BACS was

8″. Many micros use 5.25″ discs and the choice of computer was limited to those with an 8″ floppy disc drive.

The model of computer that was chosen had the facility to have up to three simultaneous users so that the two main personnel departments could also be connected to the system at a future date.

The visual display unit (VDU) was purchased separately. The division was well aware of the controversy surrounding the operation of VDUs and, given the amount of data which would have to be input to the computer, it was felt that the additional expense of a well designed and engineered screen and keyboard would be worthwhile.

The choice of printer was determined by its greatest usage: printing payslips. Capable of operating at either 250 characters per second or at 125 characters per second the printer was quick enough at the faster speed to produce payslips in a reasonable period of time and, although not 'letter quality', it could also at the slower speed produce reports that were presentable.

The present cost of the basic installation is shown in Figure 37 opposite.

Additional equipment has since been purchased to enhance the system and this is described on page 94.

Introducing the new system

The deadline set for the introduction of the new system was the first payroll of the 1982–83 tax year, ie for the month of April 1982. By that time the payroll programs and the basic accounting reports had to be completed. At least two parallel runs of the payroll were required before April. It was felt that parallel running of the new payroll system was essential, being such a sensitive area. However it was expected that the personnel enquiry programs would not be completed until later in the year.

The first problem was to load the basic records on to the new system. Working on the old computer adage of 'Garbage In, Garbage Out' it was decided not to load all the information held on the existing system on to the new one as it was clear that much of it was out of date. Instead only the basic payroll data (salaries, tax codes, National Insurance numbers, home addresses etc) were loaded. Existing manual personnel records continued to be maintained at this stage.

Figure 37
Summary of equipment and costs – integrated system

Hardware

COMPUTER	£ 8100	(including 20mb Winchester disc and MP/M operating system)
VDU	£ 850	(15″ screen)
PRINTER	£ 1660	(dual speed)
MISC.	£ 85	(cables, electric plugs etc. and initial supply of ribbons and floppy discs)
Hardware total	£10695	

Software

PAYPER	£1500	(Payroll, Personnel and SSP package at selling price)
BACSCOPY	£ 150	(for producing a floppy disc for BACS)
WORDSTAR	£ 415	(word processing package)
BASIC programming language	£ 225	(for writing extra programs)
Software total	£2290	

(Prices shown as at October 1983, excluding VAT)

This exercise showed one area where a human being was more cost efficient than the silicon chip! It proved far cheaper and faster to print the information from the old computer system and key it into the new one than to have the data transferred electronically since special programs would have had to be written. For approximately 1,000 employees it took 80 hours to key the basic information in, at a cost of £300.

After each of the two parallel runs the salaries office meticulously checked the printouts from the new programs with the actual payroll and not only did this pick up 'bugs' but also any incorrect keying of payroll information.

The first payroll using the new system was run in April 1982. The changeover from the old equipment to the new went very smoothly and the parallel running proved worthwhile. The salaries department did not receive any complaints from either companies or employees about mistakes due to incorrect programming or keying in of data.

During the following months the personnel enquiry programs, a number of standard reports and tax year end routines were added.

The amount of time required to load the remaining personnel data was considerably underestimated. It had been assumed that this information would be loaded onto the records system in small batches. This process proved to be very time consuming and other demands on the personnel management meant that no progress was made. To complete the exercise the division subsequently employed a temporary assistant to collate personnel information from the existing manual records and key the data into the system.

Facilities available on the new payroll/personnel system

STORAGE OF DATA

The information about each employee is held on 11 screens of data each receiving and/or displaying different sets of information. The screens are as follows:

1	Basic information
2 & 3	Payroll data
4	Leave record
5	Temporary amendments to payroll
6	Personnel information
7	Management development information

8   Sickness absence and statutory sick pay information

9   Cumulative payroll values

10 & 11   History records.

If data is to be added or amended the new values are input directly on to the screen. Changes are logged by the system for printing later as a control and as an audit trail. If appropriate, the history records are automatically updated.

ACCESS TO THE RECORDS

Unauthorized access to the system is prevented by a combination of user names and passwords. User access to particular screens and records is also controlled by this facility.

Individual records are brought up on to the screen, either by entering a payroll number or a surname. The system is configured so that only the salaries department staff are able to amend payroll information. Personnel management have access to these screens but cannot amend any payroll records; however they can amend other types of information. Personnel management have access to records only in their own sector of the division and do not have access to senior managers' records.

STANDARD REPORTS

A number of standard reports have been programmed into the system. These are mainly used for accounting, either by the company accountants or by the salaries department.

ADHOC ENQUIRIES

In addition to simply being able to look up the information relating to a particular individual, the personnel enquiry system enables records to be selected according to parameters specified by the user. For example, selecting all the employees of a particular company who joined after a given date and are not members of the pension scheme. After these individuals have been selected a number of options are available. For instance the

93

selected employees' records can be examined on the VDU or a printed copy can be produced. It is also possible to create a file of the selected information which is outside of the payroll/personnel system. This file can then be accessed by the user's own computer program or by a word processing system. This facility is particularly useful as information such as the salaries or home addresses of all the employees selected can be transferred to the file.

PAYROLL

In addition to having the facility for more than one payroll it is also possible to run trial payroll for checking the payslips of all employees or those employees whose payroll details have been amended since the last payroll. Payments from the main payroll run can be made directly to employees' bank accounts using BACS. The main payroll run also provides information for standard financial reports.

AMENDMENTS TO PAYE AND CODED INFORMATION

In order to save space on the information screens many of the data fields have numerical codes. For printed output where the information needs to be included in full, separate table files are used. The user has access to these files to amend and update them. Similarly, PAYE tax bands and percentages, National Insurance percentages and pension codes and percentages are kept on table files so that the user can update them without any involvement from computer programming staff.

Additional equipment purchased

FOR REMOTE USE OF THE SYSTEM

To enable the personnel departments situated at two branch locations to have direct access to the computer, modems and additional VDUs have been bought.

VDUs in the branch offices can be connected to the computer

using the public telephone system. At each of the three offices a special telephone and a modem was required so that information can be passed to and from the computer and the VDUs using the telephone circuit.

The cost of the equipment was as follows:

Modems	(3 @ £640)	£1920
VDUS	(2 @ £850)	£1700
Installation of modems	(3 @ £60)	£ 180
Installation of telephones	(3 @ £90)	£ 270
	Total	£4070

TO IMPROVE THE WORD PROCESSING FACILITY

To make the word processing package easier to operate and to produce 'letter quality' documents a second VDU with a keyboard especially configured for that package and a second printer have been purchased.

The costs were as follows:

VDU/special keyboard		£1200
Letter quality printer		£ 725
	Total	£1925

Maintenance

EQUIPMENT

All of the equipment, except the modems, were covered by a single maintenance contract. The contract provided for three preventative maintenance visits each year and for engineering cover during normal working hours. Total cost for the year commencing 1st April 1983 was £1,723.

The modems are maintained under a separate yearly contract at a cost of £69 each.

PROGRAMMING

Although changes in tax bands, National Insurance rates etc are entered by divisional staff, maintenance is required to take account of changes in legislation, such as the statutory sick pay (SSP). These updates, and any amendments or extensions to the system are provided by the programming company at an agreed rate.

6 :: Case study – personnel records system

Introduction

The organization that is the subject of this case study is a division of the UK subsidiary of an American corporation. The division employs 380 staff on a single site and they are involved with the manufacture of communications equipment. The personnel function is a corporate service to the division and is independent of any departmental groupings. The staff comprises:

personnel manager
recruitment and training manager
welfare assistant
compensation assistant
clerk/typist.

Payroll is run on an outside bureau and statutory sick pay is administered by the payroll system. Pensions are administered by a completely separate department.

Reasons for computerizing

At the time the project was initiated, early in 1982, there were three file systems in use:

personnel details
salary summary file (for administering salary information)
absenteeism/holidays/sickness etc.

These file systems were quite adequate when dealing with single enquiries but the personnel officers were being asked increasingly to provide information on a departmental or sub-group basis. In addition, the information required was becoming more complex and the provision of this and statistical reports was becoming more and more difficult and time consuming. A further complication was the increasing involvement in training, compensation and salary surveys.

Requirements of a new system

A computer based system would be required to perform accurately and quickly any selection and enquiry tasks and to provide the basis of an enhanced personnel service. The current salary system could provide details of SSP and absence records but was unable to produce summaries. The new system was required to do this and to provide an absenteeism tracking service.

The division was expanding and this was giving rise to an unacceptable work load on those responsible for dealing with job applications. The obvious answer was to utilize a word processing system for standard letters, replying to applicants, inviting them to interviews and offering employment. The central word processing facility was tried but it proved impossible to be able to guarantee access to it. Additionally, there were grave problems of loss of confidentiality. Consequently, it was decided to include word processing as a requirement of the new system.

Alternatives

Several options were explored, ranging from a main-frame to a micro-computer. The American parent company has a large main-frame in Illinois with a world wide communications network linked into it. The first option, then, was to set up a personnel database on the main-frame and link into it via the corporation's network. Three difficulties arose. First there was the potential legal problem of transmitting personnel information across national boundaries. Although data protection laws are in their infancy, it was a problem that could not be ignored. Secondly, there would be no guarantee of data security or confidentiality. And thirdly, the main-frame seemed to be unobtainable for significant lengths of time. The main-frame approach was rejected.

The UK company has a large operation in Scotland employing 1,400 people, many of whom work on the continuous 3-shift system. They have a mini-computer on which they keep extensive personnel details using a system written specially for them by a local computer software company. They were keen to extend the use of this system to other divisions within UK but it was felt that the specialist nature of the system and its cost made it unsuitable. The purchase price and first year costs would have been in the range £15,000–£20,000.

The services of a bureau were investigated but were discounted for reasons of expense. The only logical alternative remaining was a micro-computer but nobody in the personnel function knew anything about them. The division's management information services were too busy to help (and also were unfamiliar with micros) and the personnel officers approached the finance department who were already using a micro. This proved to be a valuable experience since a base knowledge of micros was attained. However, it was clear that it would be wrong just to buy a micro and expect it to run a personnel system without a good deal of effort being expended in learning how to use it. Consequently, it was decided to seek help from outside the organization.

Defining the system

A local company, specializing in micro-based personnel systems, was engaged to draw up a detailed specification for discussion. The company was told in outline what was required, ie how the system was to be used, what reports would be required, etc. Particular emphasis was placed on providing a system that would not require the users to undergo extensive training.

The software company produced a report that set out a proposed system structure together with a costed listing of hardware and software requirements. The costings proved very salutary since it would have been very easy to overlook many of the necessary pieces of hardware such as printer sheet feeders and acoustic hoods.

The original proposal was based on a dual floppy disc system but the software company strongly advised the division to await the availability of a hard disc facility for the recommended computer. This advice was taken and the increased flexibility and speed of response has fully justified the comparatively small extra cost.

The proposed software was based on a generalized database system. Some customization was required and the computer software company was asked to carry out this programming. This proved very necessary since the personnel officers did not have the time to learn the required programming skills.

An alternative quotation was sought from a second computer software company who already had links with the division. Their report showed that they did not understand the particular requirements of the personnel function and it was decided to proceed with the original company along the lines of their report.

Installing the system

The personnel officers were determined that the new system would be as useful as possible from the moment it was installed. The structure of the database and the approximate format of the data fields had already been agreed and during the first two days after delivery small amounts of data were entered in order to practice using the system.

The original intention had been to hire temporary staff to input all the data. However a trial experiment showed that too many inaccuracies were produced since the temporary staff did not have any commitment to the system. Consequently, the personnel officer most concerned with the system undertook the task herself, fitting it in with her other work. Approximately 300 partial records were completed within five days. The data chosen for this trial involved 10 of the 30 data fields on the system.

The computer software company assisted on site for the first two days and thereafter gave help and advice over the telephone. After two weeks they returned to provide a more advanced course on how to use the database. The extra facilities included selecting, sorting and generating reports.

The system was now ready to be fully operational and within a further six weeks all the base details had been loaded. In addition, work proceeded on familiarization with the word processing facility and on the setting up of the sub-system for recruitment tracking.

Use of the system

The system is in continual use providing a real service to the personnel function. Regular reports include:

weekly headcount by department (for departmental managers)
summary of leavers (for senior management)
salary survey information
training board returns.

A key issue for the division concerns salary planning and the personnel function is now in a position to provide management with an analysis of employees' salaries within the grading bands and a detailed breakdown of earnings and salary histories.

The salaries department provide full details of absenteeism, holidays taken and sickness. The personnel department are now accumulating these details against individuals with a view to producing an end-of-year summary for each department. Since this data is now on their micro-computer they can respond much more quickly than the payroll system to requests for summaries of attendance records.

This type of service provided by the micro-computer system has in turn helped the personnel function to offer a greatly improved service to the division and its management.

The word processing facility has proved invaluable in the provision of standard replies to letters. Not only has it been more efficient but also the personnel officer concerned can now devote more time to her work involving personal contact with the employees.

A novel use of the system has been the provision of a profile of employees' addresses so that discussions could be held with the local bus company concerning services and timetables. This was particularly useful when the division decided to move to another area of the town.

Summary of equipment and costs

Figure 38 sets out the hardware and software supplied with the system.

Figure 38
Summary of equipment and costs – personnel records system

Hardware

COMPUTER	£ 3995	(including 10mb Winchester disc, VDU and MS-DOS operating system)
PRINTER	£ 1660	(letter quality)
SHEET FEEDER	£ 630	(for single sheets)
STATIONERY FEEDER	£ 165	(for continuous stationery)
ACOUSTIC HOOD	£ 395	
MISCELLANEOUS	£ 225	(discs, ribbons, stationery etc.)
Hardware total	£ 7070	

Software

DATABASE PACKAGE	£ 495	
WORD PROCESSING	£ 390	
SET-UP AND TRAINING	£ 1500	
Software total	£ 2385	
TOTAL purchase cost (October 1983 prices)	£ 9455	

Extensions to the system

The international corporation offer an electronic mailing system over the communications network. The personnel department would like to link into this and could use some of the special terminals that have been installed within the division. However, they have decided to make use of their micro-computer and, to achieve this, they will purchase a communications package and link into the network via a modem.

Manpower and salary planning is another area of interest to the personnel department. There are very sophisticated (and expensive) specialist packages on the market but the division will proceed more cautiously by purchasing a standard spreadsheet package. These all-purpose planning tools are easy to use and do not require any programming skills.

Glossary of computer terms

Accumulator	transitional storage register inside a computer
Arithmetic and logic unit (ALU)	part of computer that carries out mathematical and other processing functions
Address	storage position inside a computer (also location)
Algorithm	a mathematical technique for solving a problem
Binary number	number to the base 2, eg 101011 (43 in base 10)
Bit	binary digit, either 0 or 1
Byte	a grouping of 8 bits, the smallest representational unit in a computer
Capacity	the number of program instructions or pieces of data that can be stored on a computer device
Central processing unit (CPU)	the main part of the computer containing the ALU, control unit and memory elements
Computer peripheral	a piece of computer hardware other than the central processing unit
Control unit	the part of the computer that manages all the other parts

Decimal numbers	numbers to the base 10, eg 43
Floppy disc	a thin magnetized plastic disc used for the removable permanent storage of programs and data
Function	facility that the computer has, eg ADD (two numbers) (also operator)
Hardware	the solid parts of a computer eg VDU, disc
Hard disc	an enclosed disc unit used for the permanent storage of programs and data
Input device	the piece of computer hardware through which data etc. is entered, eg VDU, cassette tape
KB (or K)	kilobyte—1,000 bytes
Location	see Address
Main-frame	a very large computer
mb	megabyte—1,000,000 bytes
Memory	the storage section of a computer
Micro-computer	a small computer whose main operational functions are carried out by a single micro-processor
Mini-computer	a medium sized computer
Modem	modulator/de-modulator, a machine for coding and decoding computer messages for transmission over the telephone system
Operand	the set of addresses containing the entities to be operated on by a function
Operating system	the control program that makes the program work

Operator	see Function
Output device	the piece of computer hardware through which data is transmitted to the user, eg VDU, cassette tape printer
Program	a set of program instructions that together make the computer perform a complete operation
Program instruction	an order to the computer to carry out a task, eg 'ADD X and Y'
RAM	Random access memory—the part of memory available to the user for his programs and data
Response time	the time taken between issuing an instruction to a computer and receiving confirmation that the instruction has been carried out
ROM	Read only memory—the part of memory that stores the operating system and other built in functions
Silicon chip	a piece of silicon on which are etched paths of electrical conduction
Software	programs and operating systems
Store	parts of a computer (see Memory) or peripheral that stores data or programs
Visual display unit (VDU)	a television type monitor that is used to control a computer and to input, examine and output data
Word	a group of bits, the smallest operational unit in a computer
Word processor	a computer dedicated to the manipulation of text

Bibliography

Personnel Books

IVE Tony. *Personnel computer systems.* London, McGraw-Hill, 1982.

WILLE Edgar *and* HAMMOND Valerie. *The Computer in Personnel Work.* Institute of Personnel Management, 1981.

PAGE G Terry, *ed. Computers in personnel: papers for the First National Conference and Exhibition on Computers in Personnel.* London, Institute of Manpower Studies/Institute of Personnel Management, 1982.

PAGE G Terry, *ed. Computers in personnel: 'Towards the personnel office of the future'. Published in association with the 2nd National Conference and Exhibition on Computers in Personnel, 12–14 July 1983.* Brighton, Institute of Manpower Studies *and* London, Institute of Personnel Management, 1983.

Computer Books

CAREY David. *How it works . . . the computer.* Ladybird books, 1979.

CURRAN Susan *and* CURNOW Ray. *The Penguin computing book.* Penguin Books, 1983.

Computer magazines

Mind Your Own Business (Cairnmark Limited)

Practical Computing (Electrical Electronic Press)

Which Computer (EMAP)